POEMS OF MANY YEARS

Edmund Blunden

POEMS OF MANY YEARS

COLLINS

ST JAMES'S PLACE, LONDON

1957

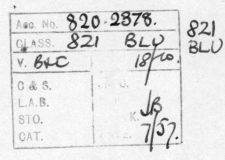

PRINTED IN GREAT BRITAIN
COLLINS CLEAR-TYPE PRESS: LONDON AND GLASGOW

To

A. C. W. EDWARDS
of Christ's Hospital

"The Tower" was first published in *The Face of England*, a collection of sketches in prose and verse by Edmund Blunden published by Messrs. Longmans Green & Co. to whom the Editor expresses his thanks for permission to include it in this book.

CONTENTS

7

8

11

PREFACE

FORTY YEARS and more have passed since the editor of
The Blue, now Sir John Woods, accepted a poem of mine
for publication. Since then I have not spent any considerable
period without impulses of verse, and I have sometimes
answered them in defiance of other concerns; the result
has been indeed a large accumulation chiefly of short pieces.
Many were gathered in *Poems* 1914–1930 and *Poems* 1930–
1940; others appeared in the less bulky volumes *Shells by
a Stream* (1944) and *After the Bombing* (1949).

From these and other sources, including recent manu-
scripts, it is to be confessed that I tried without success to
make a selection, but authors do not generally do such things
well for their own writings belonging to many distant days
and conditions. Hence I rejoice that my publishers so
readily accepted the choice of our friend Mr. Rupert Hart-
Davis, as selector and editor of my poetry; both the
personal and the literary reasons for my rejoicing at this
are incomparable.

As the reader will readily grant, the occasion is not such
as brings only happy thoughts to an author of my age.
Many of those who were friends to my poems at the outset
are dead and gone; and I still feel my youthful lack of
understanding, for life was more generous to me than I saw.
I should like to reach S. E. Winbolt, Alan Porter, Robert
Nichols, H. J. Massingham, Eddie Marsh—to name only
those—even now, so as to let them know that their en-
couragement is not forgotten. Philip Tomlinson has now

joined them, a man whose life was one long appreciation of the poetical. Among others who favoured my beginnings and remain to read these words I venture to speak with gratitude of Siegfried Sassoon, Sir John Squire and H. M. Tomlinson; and I look out of England to Louis Bonnerot in Paris and Takeshi Saito in Tokyo for their continued kindness to such pages as these. My obligations would need many more names than I can well include now.

Sometimes it has seemed as though England might be losing the old characteristic of treating verse as a readable sort of composition, but now looking back, even looking at the moment, I am sure I observe the Common Reader still very much on the scene. He or she may have an excessive zeal for " anthology " pieces, but we who write without purposing those are still supported by such quiet idealists.

When one has read poetry for so long as I, too, have, a preface like this may be expected to include a word on the old question, what it is. Changes of professional judgment are so frequent that the answer does not grow easier. I have seen with surprise how beloved examples have abruptly become horrible examples, and how a new day blows its trumpets for writings hard to connect with what *was* poetry just before. The principal thing is still with me; poetry is as much a part of the universe as mathematics and physics. It is not a clever device or recreation, unless the Eternal is clever. Many are conscious of it as experience, though, as Hardy hints, sometimes when it was most at hand " we were looking away." In various modes of speech and impressions of metre many seek to do justice to this quality in human life. Music may have the advantage, and painting —for certain times. The method of language for conveying some perception of the grace beyond the facts is open to all: for me the essence of the blessing is often given in some melody and sidelight by an "unimportant" poet where I find the great ones marching on another objective after all.

June 1956   EDMUND BLUNDEN

THE YELLOWHAMMER

With rural admixture of shrill and sweet,
Forging his fairy fetter for the ear
Of passing folks, from pollards close the wheat,
The yellowhammer gives the sun a cheer.
  Delighted with his leafy maze
  Like dancing elves he nods and sways,
   And now trills out a chime that's fair,
   And now grates out what he might spare,
While from the totter-grass gazes the humble hare.

1916

THE FESTUBERT SHRINE

A sycamore on either side
In whose lovely leafage cried
  Hushingly the little winds—
Thus was Mary's shrine descried.

" Sixteen Hundred and Twenty-Four "
Legended above the door,
  " Pray, sweet gracious Lady, pray
For our souls,"—and nothing more.

Builded of rude gray stones and these
Scarred and marred from base to frieze
  With the shrapnel's pounces—ah,
Fair she braved War's gaunt disease:

Fair she pondered on the strange
Embitterments of latter change,
  Looking fair towards Festubert,
Cloven roof and tortured grange.

Work of carving too there was,
(Once had been her reredos),
   In this cool and peaceful cell
That the hoarse guns blared across.

Twisted oaken pillars graced
With oaken amaranths interlaced
   In oaken garlandry, had borne
Her holy niche—and now laid waste.

Mary, pray for us? O pray!
In thy dwelling by this way
   What poor folks have knelt to thee!
We are no less poor than they.

May 1916

FESTUBERT:
THE OLD GERMAN LINE

Sparse mists of moonlight hurt our eyes
   With gouged and scourged uncertainties
   Of soul and soil in agonies

One derelict grim skeleton
That drench and dry had battened on
   Still seemed to wish us malison;

Still zipped across the gouts of lead
Or cracked like whipcracks overhead;
   The gray rags fluttered on the dead.

May 1916

"TRANSPORT UP" AT YPRES

The thoroughfares that seem so dead to daylight passers-by
Change character when dark comes down, and traffic starts
    to ply;
Never a noisier street than the Rue de Malou then becomes
With the cartwheels jolting the dead awake, and the cars
    like rumbling drums.

The crazy houses watch them pass, and stammer with the
    roar,
The drivers hustle on their mules, more come behind and
    more;
Briskly the black mules clatter by, to-day was Devil's Mass;
The loathly smell of picric here, and there a touch of gas.

From silhouette to pitchy blur, beneath the bitter stars,
The interminable convoy streams of horses, vans, and cars.
They clamour through the cheerless night, the streets a
    slattern maze,
The sentries at the corners shout them on their different
    ways.

And so they go, night after night, and chance the shrapnel
    fire,
The sappers' waggons stowed with frames and concertina
    wire,
The ration-limbers for the line, the lorries for the guns:
While overhead with fleering light stare down those
    withered suns.

LES HALLES D'YPRES

A tangle of iron rods and spluttered beams,
  On brickwork past the skill of a mason to mend:
A wall with a bright blue poster—odd as dreams
  Is the city's latter end.

A shapeless obelisk looms Saint Martin's spire,
  Now a lean aiming-mark for the German guns;
And the Cloth Hall crouches beside, disfigured with fire,
  The glory of Flanders once.

Only the foursquare tower still bears the trace
  Of beauty that was, and strong embattled age,
And gilded ceremonies and pride of place—
  Before this senseless rage.

And still you may see (below the noon serene,
  The mysterious, changeless vault of sharp blue light),
The pigeons come to the tower, and flaunt and preen,
  And flicker in playful flight.

TREES ON THE CALAIS ROAD

Like mourners filing into church at a funeral,
  These droop their sombre heads and troop to the coast,
The untimely rain makes mystery round them all
  And the wind flies round them like the ghost
  That the body on the blackened trestles lost.
Miserere sobs the weary
Sky, sackclothed, stained, and dreary,
And they bend their heads and sigh
  Miserere, Miserere!

22

With natural dole and lamentation
They groan for the slaughter and desecration,
But every moment adds to the cry
Of that dead army driving by.

1917

BLEUE MAISON

Now to attune my dull soul, if I can
To the contentment of this countryside
Where man is not for ever killing man
But quiet days like these calm waters glide.
And I will praise the blue flax in the rye,
And pathway bindweed's trumpet-like attire,
Pink rest-harrow and curlock's glistening eye,
And poppies flaring like St. Elmo's fire.

And I will praise the willows silver-gray,
And where I stand the road is rippled over
With airy dreams of blossomed bean and clover,
And shyest birds come elfin-like to play:
And in the rifts of blue above the trees
Pass the full sails of natural Odysseys.

1917

THE SILVER BIRD OF HERNDYKE
MILL

By Herndyke Mill there haunts, folks tell,
   A strange and silver-breasted bird,
Her call is like a silver bell,
   So sweet a bell was never heard,—

23

The Silver Bird of Herndyke Mill,
    That flies so fast against the blast,
    And scares the stoat with one soft note—
To hear her makes a man's blood chill.

The Charnel Path behind the Church,
    When nights are blackest, makes me pause,
But there 'tis only magpies perch
    And churning owls and goistering daws,
I fear the churchyard spooks much less,
    For all their flaming, starving eyes,
    Than that same Silver Bird which flies
At times through Herndyke wilderness.

In summer time the carps and rudds
    Sun in their scores below the weir:
In winter time the hurtling floods
    Forbid a soul to venture near.
But summer time and winter time
    Few people dare to loiter there—
    Though mushrooms spring in many a ring—
For fear the Silver Bird should chime.

The stranger hears me with a smile.
    Why should a man so fear a bird?
But listen to my words awhile,
    But listen till the whole is heard;
And if your conscience is opprest
    With shameful act or wicked will,
    You durst not go to Herndyke Mill
Where flits the bird with silver breast.

Below the pleasant meeting-place
    Of deep main stream and dwindled leat,
Where flock and glint the faint-heart dace,
    By banks deep-grown in rabbit's-meat,

A little footbridge used to be—
    A single plank from bank to bank,
    A hand-rail white to see at night—
That led into a shrubbery.

In the spring the sunlight green and cool
    Dries up the seething grounds, and makes
The kingcups yet more beautiful,
    And ushers out the bright green snakes.
But no one loves the aguish mist
    That writhes its way at eventide
    Along the copse's waterside:
So rarely come they there to tryst.

No lovers loiter there; alone
    The homeless man may break the bounds,
But in the years now fled and flown
    The miller used to mind these grounds,
And sometimes on the bridge he stood
    In twilight peace, at day's decease;
    Wrapt in his thought, as one who sought
To seem at one with stream and wood.

Now as he leant upon the rail
    One glimmering summer night, when glooms
Were hearkening to the nightingale
    And lading with dim dew the blooms,
Out of the woodside quietly
    An aged woman came, not fair,
    But crowned with shining silver hair,
And craved a little charity.

" Sir, I am faint with walking far,
    And penniless, and very old,
And under my unlucky star
    I have no home, come warm or cold.

I have no sons,—my splendid son
  That was my pride and dear love died,
  Died in the war against the Tsar;
And I am friendless, loved of none."

The miller did not answer her—
  A selfish man whose god was greed.
The wandering lady cried, " Good sir,
  I pray you help me in my need."
With that the miller scorned her: " Go,
  I care not if you go to die.
  God does not help you, and should I?
Sure some great sin has brought you low."

For such harsh words she set on him
  A fearful curse, a dread reproach,
And while she said it, down the stream
  In darkness splashed a chub or roach.
" I go to die within your wood,
  My silver hair shall tarnish there;
  And by God's word a silver bird
Shall spring therefrom, the bird of Good.

The silver locks that care has made
  Shall turn into a silver breast—
The bird of Good shall never fade,
  Here shall she fly, and here shall rest.
If evil men come near her grange
  She shall affright them with her sweet
  Monotony of notes, and beat
Her wings about them fair and strange.

The holy presence of God shall awe
  The evil-doer that passes here.
From your white mill, and your green shaw,
  Shall spring a rumour sped with fear.

The Silver Bird, God's messenger,
  Shall guard the shrine of things divine,
  And your foul lie shall never die
While men are left that looked on her."

Her words were keen and sharp as flints:
  The miller stood as carved in stone.
She ceased: the silence made him wince,
  He looked and found himself alone.
A rustling in the tenterhooks
  Of brambles told him where she went,
  And with that rustling softly blent
The ripple-dripple of the brooks.

The little greenish stars looked on,
  The rustling in the coppice died;
A bat swerved oddly and was gone,
  A half-awakened night-wind sighed,
The miller with his heavy tread
  Was nearly to his threshold yew,
  A dor flew by with crackling cry
And struck him with a sort of dread.

The morning trod the dews once more
  And led abroad the rookery:
The pigeons glistened round the door,
  The wheel rolled round contentedly.
Free went the miller's callous tongue:
  He had forgot the wanderer's curse,
  Or else he found himself no worse;
And warm the sunlight was, and young.

And so he went his wonted ways
  And robbed the farmer when he could,
And it was many many days
  Before he walked into his wood.

But in the sighing of the year,
    The shocked-up sheaves and withered leaves,
    The mourning nooks and sullen brooks
Brought back the woman's menace clear.

The sallows, how they shake and swirl
    As chilled by Autumn's trembling hands,
Their yellowed leaves so spin and twirl
    That down they drop like wasted brands.
They clog and huddle in the stream
    That's ruffled with the dismal draught
    Until their golden foundered craft
Are jostled by the groping bream.

There seems no heart in wood or wide,
    The midday comes with twilight fears,
The winds along the coverside
    Pause like bewildered travellers—
The miller picked his gloomy way,
    Intent to hound from off his ground
    A travelling man whose caravan
In cover of the coppice lay.

The sighing of the year was borne
    Deep, deep into the miller's soul.
The very footbridge looked forlorn,
    And *plop* plunged in a startled vole.
What shadows made his fancy grim
    Born of the outcast woman's word—
    When suddenly a silver bird
Was hovering, calling over him.

Her chiming channelled through his brain,
    Her bright eyes held him, spelled him there.
He struck at her, he struck in vain,
    She fluttered round him, strange and fair.

And with her was that holy power
  So pure-intense as stilled his sense
  And in his ears the voice of tears
Grew slowly like a mournful flower.

The daylight dwindled from his eyes,
  A haze grew on him filled with moan;
His dazed soul stumbled with surmise,
  He walked the wilds of fear alone.
O who can tell what dreadful days
  He seemed to pass in this wild spell,
  Through what intolerable hell
Of phantoms with their searching gaze!

At last from glooms the silver breast
  Took fashion, and the dull day's light
Was round him (never light so blest),
  And then the Silver Bird took flight.
O miller, see your punishment,
  Your golden gain has brought forth pain,
  Your spoutsman's-boy has more of joy
Whose poor wage means his mother's rent.

Now, many a month and many a year
  Has died away on holt and hill
Since that rich miser told his fear
  And fled away and shut the mill.
And such stark tales have come to me
  Whom neighbours call Poor Poaching Jack
  As every time have turned me back
From footing Herndyke shrubbery.

I've shot down pheasants from their roost
  By moonlight in the woods of squires:
In open day I've often noosed
  The vicar's pike with cunning wires.

29

I've fooled a hundred keepers round,
　Risked Redstone Gaol and did not fail;
　But yon woodside I never tried
For fear of that which guards the ground.

The waters underneath the weir
　Hold battening monstrous fish by shoals:
And if a man is conscience-clear
　He well may come with baits and trolls;
And sure his creel would soon be full
　If, fearless of the bird of good,
　He angled all along the wood,
And in the blackness of the pool.

And nettles bunch where pansies flowered
　Within the garden's gap-struck pale,
And where the mill-wheel's spouting showered
　The weedy waters wellnigh fail:
And resolute wasps come year by year
　Through bank's warm clay to make their way
　And build their nests, whence on their quests
Throughout the little garth they steer.

Among those twisted apple trees
　The little sunlights do abound:
They burn along like yellow bees
　And chequer all the shadowy ground:
The golden nobs and pippins swell
　And all unnoticed waste their prime,
　For a few folk love to hear the chime
That brings the world of woe pell-mell.

By Herndyke Mill there haunts, folks tell,
　A holy silver-breasted bird;
Her call is like a silver bell,
　So sweet a bell was never heard,

The Silver Bird of Herndyke Mill,
   That flies so fast, against the blast,
   And frights the stoat with one soft note—
To hear her makes a man's blood chill.

January–March 1916

THE WAGGONER

The old waggon drudges through the miry lane,
   By the skulking pond where the pollards frown,
Notched dumb surly images of pain;
   On a dulled earth the night droops down.

Wincing to slow and wistful airs
   The leaves on the shrubbed oaks know their hour,
And the unknown wandering spoiler bares
   The thorned black hedge of a mournful shower.

Small bodies fluster in the dead brown wrack
   As the stumbling shaft-horse jingles past
And the waggoner flicks his whip a crack;
   The odd light flares on shadows vast

Over the lodges and oasts and byres
   Of the darkened farm; the moment hangs wan
As though nature flagged and all desires.
   But in the dim court the ghost is gone

From the hug-secret yew to the penthouse wall
   And stooping there seems to listen to
The waggoner leading the gray to stall,
   As centuries past itself would do.

1919

ALMSWOMEN

At Quincey's moat the squandering village ends,
And there in the almshouse dwell the dearest friends
Of all the village, two old dames that cling
As close as any trueloves in the spring.
Long, long ago they passed three-score-and-ten,
And in this doll's-house lived together then;
All things they have in common being so poor,
And their one fear, Death's shadow at the door.
Each sundown makes them mournful, each sunrise
Brings back the brightness in their failing eyes.

How happy go the rich fair-weather days
When on the roadside folk stare in amaze
At such a honeycomb of fruit and flowers
As mellows round their threshold; what long hours
They gloat upon their steepling hollyhocks,
Bee's balsams, feathery southernwood and stocks,
Fiery dragon's-mouths, great mallow leaves
For salves, and lemon-plants in bushy sheaves,
Shagged Esau's-hands with five green finger-tips.
Such old sweet names are ever on their lips.

As pleased as little children where these grow
In cobbled pattens and worn gowns they go,
Proud of their wisdom when on gooseberry shoots
They stuck egg shells to fright from coming fruits
The brisk-billed rascals; scanning still to see
Their neighbour owls saunter from tree to tree,
Or in the hushing half-light mouse the lane
Long-winged and lordly.
                        But when those hours wane
Indoors they ponder, scared by the harsh storm
Whose pelting saracens on the window swarm,

And listen for the mail to clatter past
And church clock's deep bay withering on the blast;
They feed the fire that flings its freakish light
On pictured kings and queens grotesquely bright,
Platters and pitchers, faded calendars
And graceful hourglass trim with lavenders.

Many a time they kiss and cry and pray
That both be summoned in the selfsame day,
And wiseman linnet tinkling in his cage
End too with them the friendship of old age,
And all together leave their treasured room
Some bell-like evening when the May's in bloom.

1920

THE PIKE

From shadows of rich oaks outpeer
The moss-green bastions of the weir,
Where the quick dipper forages
In elver-peopled crevices.
And a small runlet trickling down the sluice
Gossamer music tires not to unloose.

Else round the broad pool's hush
Nothing stirs.
Unless sometime a straggling heifer crush
Through the thronged spinney whence the pheasant whirs;
Or martins in a flash
Come with wild mirth to dip their magical wings,
While in the shallow some doomed bulrush swings
At whose hid root the diver vole's teeth gnash.

And nigh this toppling reed, still as the dead
  The great pike lies, the murderous patriarch,
  Watching the waterpit shelving and dark
Where through the plash his lithe bright vassals thread.

    The rose-finned roach and bluish bream
    And staring ruffe steal up the stream
    Hard by their glutted tyrant, now
    Still as a sunken bough.

      He on the sandbank lies,
        Sunning himself long hours
      With stony gorgon eyes:
        Westward the hot sun lowers.

Sudden the gray pike changes, and quivering poises for
    slaughter;
  Intense terror wakens around him, the shoals scud awry,
    but there chances
    A chub unsuspecting; the prowling fins quicken, in fury
  he lances;
And the miller that opens the hatch stands amazed at the
  whirl in the water.

1919

SHEEPBELLS

    Moonsweet the summer evening locks
      The lips of babbling day:
    Mournfully, most mournfully
      Light dies away.

    There the yew, the solitary,
    Vaults a deeper melancholy,

As from distant bells
Chance music wells
From the browsing-bells.

Thus they dingle, thus they chime,
    While the woodlark's dimpling rings
In the dim air climb;
In the dim and dewy loneness
Where the woodlark sings.

1916

THE UNCHANGEABLE

Though I within these two last years of grace
Have seen bright Ancre scourged to brackish mire,
And meagre Belgian becks by dale and chace
Stamped into sloughs of death with battering fire—
Spite of all this, I sing you high and low,
My old loves, Waters, be you shoal or deep,
Waters whose lazy continual flow
Learns at the drizzling weir the tongue of sleep.
For Sussex cries from primrose lags and brakes,
" Why do you leave my woods untrod so long?
Still float the bronze carp on my lilied lakes,
Still the wood-fairies round my spring wells throng;
And chancing lights on willowy waterbreaks
Dance to the bubbling brooks of elfin song."

1917

A WATERPIECE

The wild-rose bush lets loll
Her sweet-breathed petals on the pool,
The bream-pool overshadowed with the cool
Of oaks where myriad mumbling wings patrol.

There the live dimness burrs with droning glees
Of hobby-horses with their starting eyes
And violet humble-bees and dizzy flies;
That from the dewsprings drink the honeyed lees.

Up the slow stream the immemorial bream
(For when had Death dominion over them?)
Through green pavilions of ghost leaf and stem,
A conclave of blue shadows in a dream,
Glide on; idola that forgotten plan,
Incomparably wise, the doom of man.

1919

A COUNTRY GOD

When groping farms are lanterned up
    And stolchy ploughlands hid in grief,
And glimmering byroads catch the drop
    That weeps from sprawling twig and leaf,
And heavy-hearted spins the wind
    Among the tattered flags of Mirth,—
Then who but I flit to and fro,
With shuddering speech, with mope and mow,
    And glass the eyes of Earth?

Then haunt I by some moanish brook
  Where lank and snaky brambles swim,
Or where the hill pines swarthy look
  I whirry through the dark and hymn
A dull-voiced dirge and threnody,
  An echo of the world's sad drone
That now appals the friendly stars—
O wail for blind brave youth whose wars
  Turn happiness to stone.

How rang the cavern-shades of old
  To my melodious pipes, and then
My bright-haired bergamask patrolled
  Each lawn and plot for laughter's din:
Never a sower flung broad cast,
  No hedger brished nor scythesman swung,
Nor maiden trod the purpling press
But I was by to guard and bless
  And for their solace sung.

But now the sower's hand is writhed
  In livid death, the bright rhythm stolen,
The gold grain flattened and unscythed,
  The boars in the vineyard gnarled and sullen
Havocking the grapes; and the pouncing wind
  Spins the spattered leaves of the glen
In a mockery dance, death's hue-and-cry;
With all my murmurous pipes flung by
  And summer not to come again.

1918

THE SIGHING TIME

The sighing time, the sighing time! . . .
  The old house mourns and shudders so;
  And the bleak garrets' crevices
  Like whirring distaffs utter dread;
  Streams of shadow people go
  By hollow stairs and passages
  In black cloths herding out their dead.
  Along the creaking corridors
  They troop with sighs, grayhead and young,
  They droop their heads in bitter tears.
  The panels yawn like charnel doors
  Where the dark windows ivy-clung
  Are gloating spiders' belvederes.
  Without, like old Laocoön,
  The yewtree claws the serpent gusts,
  The wicket swings with peacock screams.
  Time in the courtyard leans upon
  His pausing scythe, in dim mistrusts
  And sad recalls of summer dreams.
  The garden, cynically sown
  With leaves in death unlovely, bows
  Its tragic plume of pipy stalks:
  Poison-spores have overgrown
  In crazy-coloured death-carouse
  The parterres and the lovers' walks.
  The anguished sun is swiftly set,
  And Hesper's primrose coronal
  Is sullied with distortions pale.
  The grange bell in its minaret
  With dreary three-times-dreary call
    Dingles in the gale.
The sighing time, the sighing time.

1917

38

IN FESTUBERT

Now every thing that shadowy thought
  Lets peer with bedlam eyes at me
From alley ways and thoroughfares
  Of cynic and ill memory
Lifts a gaunt head, sullenly stares,
  Shuns me as a child has shunned
A whizzing dragonfly that daps
  Above his mudded pond.

Now bitter frosts, muffling the morn
  In old days, crunch the grass anew;
There where the floods made fields forlorn
  The glinzy ice grows thicker through.
The pollards glower like mummies when
  Thieves break into a pyramid,
Inscrutable as those dead men
  With painted mask and balm-cloth hid;

And all the old delight is cursed
  Redoubling present undelight.
Splinter, crystal, splinter and burst;
  And sear no more with second sight.

1916

MONT DE CASSEL

Here on the sunnier scarp of the hill let us rest,
And hoard the hastening hour,
Find a mercy unexpressed
In the chance wild flower

39

We may find on the pathway side, or the glintering flint,
Or other things so small and unregarded:
Descry far windows fired with the sun, to whom
Nothing is small or mean.
To us, let the war be a leering ghost now shriven,
And as though it had never been;
A tragedy mask discarded.
A lamp in a tomb.
What though in the hounded east, now we are gone,
The thunder-throated cannonade boom on?
Too long we have striven,
Too soon we return.
The white stone roads go valleyward from the height,
Like our hopes, to be lost in haze
Where the bonfires burn
With the dross of summer days—
(Our summer hideous, harvesting affright).
Ah, see the silver Spirit dream among his quiet dells,
Hear the slow slumbrous bells,
The voices of a world long by,
Come dim and clear and dim
As the wheat-leys sleep or sigh.
Fall into musings thence, let Psyche stray
Where she lists,
Among small things of little account,
Or through the coloured mists;—
Myriad the roads to the visionary mount,
And the white forehead of the Mystery.
    But alas, she falls in a swoon,
    Pale-lipped like a withering moon;
So terrible is the insistency
Of the east where like a fiend automaton
The thunder-throated cannonade booms on.

September 1917

40

THE BARN

I

Rain-sunken roof, grown green and thin
For sparrows' nests and starlings' nests·
Dishevelled eaves; unwieldy doors,
Cracked rusty pump, and oaken floors,
And idly-pencilled names and jests
    Upon the posts within.

The light pales at the spider's lust,
The wind tangs through the shattered pane:
An empty hop-poke spreads across
The gaping frame to mend the loss
And keeps out sun as well as rain,
    Mildewed with clammy dust.

The smell of apples stored in hay
And homely cattle-cake is there.
Use and disuse have come to terms,
The walls are hollowed out by worms,
But men's feet keep the mid-floor bare
    And free from worse decay.

II

A man was lying in the straw
That hid him wholly but his head.
The face was not an English face,
But hinted of some Southern race.
The eyes seemed strained, the eyes seemed dead.
    A farm boy came and saw.

He thought it was some gipsy man
Had crawled in there to sleep the night:
He cried to him to send him out,
The form lay still despite his shout:
He went, and saw his face dead white.
        Fear touched him, and he ran.

He found the farmer in the yard,
Breathlessly he told the tale;
The farmer looked him scornfully,
But yet he went himself to see.
He saw and turned a little pale,
        And drew his breath in hard,

And trudged away without a word
Into the infield, where he told
The aged ditcher what had come:
The old man paused a moment, dumb,
Then muttered, " Was he very cold? "
        " Cold as a frost-clammed bird."

" Then did you touch his face and feel? "
The farmer scanned the shrewd gray eyes
But read small meaning there, and said,
" I did, to see if he was dead."
The answer struck him with surprise,
        " It will not work you weal."

" That is no man that's lying chill
And huddled dead-like in the straw;
But I maun see the thing myself,
For I am feared it is an elf
That bodes no good for fold and shaw
        And hops upon your hill."

The two men turned, and back they tramped,
Back to the barn, and both went in;
The dusty sunlight flickered on
A face all sallow under wan,
Evilly puckered and pinched and thin.
    A curse from the stark eyes lamped.

The old bowed ditcher stretched a hand
And clutched the farmer's shoulder, " See,
Its eyes are worse than any ghost's,
They mean to curse your ricks and oasts.
Yon is a devil—let it be,
    But it will harm your land."

And even while he spoke, the face
Had vanished, and the straw sank down.
The odd ducks clacked beside the pond,
The cocks crowed sleepily from beyond
The staddles of the hayrick brown.
    The thing had left no trace.

III

The hoptime came with sun and shower
That made the hops hang hale and good;
The village swarmed with motley folk,
Far through the morning calm awoke
Noise of the toiling multitude
    Who stripped the tall bines' bower.

Slatternly folk from sombre streets
And crowded courts like narrow wells
Are picking in that fragrant air;
Gipsies with jewelled fingers there
Gaze dark, speak low, their manner tells
    Of thievings and deceits.

43

And country dames with mittened wrists,
Grandams and girls and mothers stand
And stretch the bine-head on the bin,
And deftly jerk the loosed hops in.
Black stains the never-resting hand
    So white for springtide trysts.

And by and by the little boys,
Tired with the work and women's talk,
Make slyly off, and run at large
Down to the river, board the barge
Roped in to shore, and stand to baulk
    The bargee's angry noise:

While through the avenues of hops
The measurers and the poke-boys go.
The measurers scoop the heaved hops out,
While gaitered binmen move about
With sharpened hopdog, at whose blow
    The stubborn cluster drops.

Such was the scene that autumn morn,
But when the dryer in his oast
Had loaded up his lattice-floors,
He called a binman at the doors,
" We want no more; the kilns are closed.
    Bid measurer blow the horn."

The binman found the measurer pleased,
For hops were clean and work was through;
He told him what the dryer said,
The measurer nodded his gray head,
Lifted the battered horn and blew.
    And so the day's work ceased.

It was but noon; the pickers went.
The farmer and the measurer met.
Both praised the hops that morning got,
The farmer said, " So this is what
The barn ghost brings, no trouble yet,
    And this is all it meant."

The measurer answered, " Maybe so,
But you can speak before the crash.
The sky is getting ugly looks."
In thunder-yellow lights the rooks
Flew crowding into elm and ash
    And gloom began to grow.

The air was loud with bleating droves,
And hot and tense; the southern hills
Were crushed in cerecloths, white like steam;
The dust whirled round the homeward team,
Rain splashed the whited windowsills,
    And rustled in the groves.

Thunder and thunder came to war.
In startling suddenness vast cloud
Dropped shreds of blackness, drooped in rain
And deluged garths and hops and grain,
And lightnings plunged and madly ploughed
    Through cloudy steep and scaur.

The rainstorm harried all the vale
In steady flood, no separate drops,
Big bubbles oozed from sodden ground,
The shower-butts flowed, the dykes were drowned;
But down the valley all the hops
    Were hardly touched by hail.

The hail beset the hill alone,
And seemed to prove the farmer curst;
Jagged cruel hailstones struck the hops,
And gashed the bines from the hop-pole tops,
And eddying screaming winds outburst
  And flung the hop-poles prone.

The hope were ruined in an hour
That took the toil of many a day;
The farmer and the measurer saw
The wasting of their work with awe,
Till bright blue glittered through the gray,
  And hailstones lost their power.

This was the first of much distress
That came upon the farm; the oast
Was struck with lightning, and took fire
As if good fortune's funeral pyre.
Men whispered of the grimly ghost
  That caused the lucklessness.

Only the farmer never feared,
Though footrot ravaged all his sheep.
Redwater came and rotted most;
The shepherd muttered of the ghost,
But he with patience stern and deep
  Held on though all men jeered.

Three years of evil circumstance
And ceaseless labour left him poor;
He barely won his daily bread,
And all one autumn lay in bed
For illness taken by mischance.
  The people shunned his door.

And stray folk plundered all his fruit,
And broke his hedges into gaps:
They scoured his copses and his crofts,
And robbed his barns and apple-lofts,
While he lay in a pale collapse,
    And could not stop the loot.

Yet without care of devil or man,
And thinking straight, and fearing God,
Once more the farmer came to health,
And went to work to win back wealth,
And dared to plough and dared to plod
    The farm that all would ban.

Luck veered towards him once again;
His cobnuts in a scanty year
Were household words for many miles,
Men's faces changed from sneers to smiles,
For good and wicked wishes veer
    With pleasure and with pain.

And clearing out a lumber-room
He found a pot of golden coins,
Tarnished, yet heavy yellow gold;
There is a prize for being bold,
And scorning what the world enjoins
    With words and looks of doom.

IV

So patient courage won the day.
And when forebodings seemed fulfilled,
The hardy sceptic shook his head,
And took no note of what was said
But boldly gathered, garnered, tilled,
    And scorned to go away.

The hamlet round the striving farm
Made many gloomy prophecies.
Some feared to work upon the place,
Some told the farmer to his face
That while that house and land were his,
    They must be bound with harm.

Yet to this day the barn remains
Not brooding over fortune strange;
The drowsy sunlight creeps and crawls
In through the century-crannied walls,
And every breeze that roves the grange
    Sings in the splintered panes.

All merry noise of hens astir
Or sparrows squabbling on the roof
Comes to the barn's broad open door,
You hear upon the stable floor
Old hungry Dapple strike his hoof,
    And the blue fan-tail's whirr.

The barn is old, and very old,
But not a place of spectral fear.
Cobwebs and dust and speckling sun
Come to old buildings every one.
Long since they made their dwelling here,
    And here you may behold

Nothing but simple wane and change;
Your tread will wake no ghost, your voice
Will fall on silence undeterred.
No phantom wailing will be heard,
Only the farm's blithe cheerful noise;
    The barn is old, not strange.

The superstition dies away,
And through the minds of country men
A callous thought of life has passed,
And myth and legend-lore are cast
Far from the modern yeoman's ken,
    Fears of a bygone day.

Something is lost, perhaps: the old
Simplicity of rustic wit
Is banished by the rude disdain
And pride that speaks a boorish brain,
The pride that kills the fear of it,
    And strikes its kindness cold.

LEISURE

Listen, and lose not the sweet luring cry,
Nor let the far-off torches gleam in vain;
The moments are so few, so soon slipt by,
And yet so rare to lull the harried brain.
For now is autumn fully come, and steals
In a king's daydream over weald and wold,
And the last honey is scoured, the last sheaf housed;
    And the boon earth reveals,
With the melodious drone of plenty drowzed,
Leisure and loving-kindness manifold.

Then when the early primroses of day
Bud through the cool mist, fail O fail not then
To scan the sign of beauty, nor betray
The soul's first love that might not flower again.
And calm and marvellous the wide lands lie
Dim with awakening-notes of little birds;

And the delighted Spirit in the dells
  Wooes the sun's opening eye
With his droll night-whims, puffballs' pepper-gourds.
Startling white mushrooms and bronze chantarelles.

Gentle and dewy-bright the landscape fills
Through the serene and crystal atmosphere;
Night's blackamoors sink into reedy ghylls
To skulk unsunned till eve's pale lantern peer;
And silver elvish gossamers go dance
On twinkling voyages at the caprice
Of autumn half-asleep and idly playing
  With fancies as they chance,
The feather's fall, the doomed red leaf delaying,
And all the tiny circumstance of peace.

Along the purpled bramble-brake he treads,
The giant sauntering like a peasant boy,
Murmuring a song, brushing through russet beds
Of sunburned bracken with " Hi-gee " and " Whoi ";
Forgetting all the tumult and the toil
Of harvest, for the vale farms all are still,
Save thatchers on the yellow ricks, or where
  Smoke's light blue pennants coil
From white-coned oasts, or bonfires fume and flare,
Or flagging breezes twirl the black-vanned mill.

Now the old hedger with his half-moon-hook,
Plashing the spiked thorn, musing of bygone men,
Shakes the crab apples plopping in the brook
Till jangling wildgeese flush from the drowned fen.
Nodding he plods in his gray revery,
Self-sorry robins humouring his thought's cast;
While scarce perceived, by red walls warm with peaches,
  By bosque and signal-tree,

And otters'-lodges on the river-reaches,
The feather-footed moments tiptoe past.

Tranquilly beats the country's heart to-day,—
Golden-age-beckonings, lost pastoral things,
Fantastically near and far-away,
Stretch in the sunny calm their blazoned wings.
Then tarry, tiptoe moments, nor too soon
Let death beat down your saffron butterflies
Nor crush your gleaning autumn crocuses,
    But in a gradual swoon
Let long dreams flaunt till eve accomplishes
And round the down the tide-mist multiplies.

To-morrow's brindled shouting storms will flood
The purblind hollows with a leaden rain
And flat the gleaning-fields to choking mud
And writhe the groaning woods with bursts of pain.
What though that wrath relent ere night? the hills,
Lonely in sharp light from horizons cold,
Shall sadden, and the vapour-piercing spires,
    Where the last sunlight thrills,
Jewelling the ghostwhite city and wistful fires,
Bring tears like spent delights with tales long told.

To-morrow—but to-day, to-day is young.
Still nods the sunflower, still the church owls prey,
Nor yet has sparrow chirped nor cockerel flung
From cobwebbed rafters his third roundelay
Which is the very music of the morn.
Those hours of peaceful witchcraft are to come;
Wander we lovingly and gather store
    Of balms for griefs unborn:
Lest the far fairy eyes appeal no more,
And mercy's music be for ever dumb.

1919

MALEFACTORS

Nailed to these green laths long ago,
You cramp and shrivel into dross,
Blotched with mildews, gnawed with moss,
And now the eye can scarcely know
The snake among you from the kite,
   So sharp does Death's fang bite.

I guess your stories; you were shot
Hovering above the miller's chicks;
And you, coiled on his threshold bricks—
Hissing you died; and you, sir Stoat,
Dazzled with stableman's lantern stood
   And tasted crabtree wood.

Here then you leered-at luckless churls,
Clutched to your clumsy gibbet, shrink
To shapeless orts; hard by the brink
Of this black scowling pond that swirls
To turn the wheel beneath the mill,
   The wheel so long since still.

There's your revenge, the wheel at tether,
The miller gone, the white planks rotten,
The very name of the mill forgotten,
Dimness and silence met together.
Felons of fur and feather, can
   There lurk some crime in man,

In man your executioner,
Whom here Fate's cudgel battered down?
Did he too filch from squire and clown?

The damp gust makes the ivy whir
Like passing death; the sluices well,
    Dreary as a passing-bell.

1919

CLARE'S GHOST

Pitch-dark night shuts in, and the rising gale
    Is full of the presage of rain,
    And there comes a withered wail
    From the wainscot and jarring pane,
    And a long funeral surge
    Like a wood-god's dirge,
Like the wash of the shoreward tides, from the firs on the
    crest.

The shaking hedges blacken, the last gold flag
    Lowers from the West;
The Advent bell moans wild like a witch hag
    In the storm's unrest,
And the lychgate lantern's candle weaves a shroud,
    And the unlatched gate shrieks loud.

Up fly the smithy sparks, but are baffled from soaring
    By the pelting scurry, and ever
As puff the bellows, a multitude more outpouring
    Die foiled in the endeavour.

And a stranger stands with me here in the glow
Chinked through the door, and marks
    The sparks
Perish in whirlpool wind, and if I go
To the delta of cypress, where the glebe gate cries,

53

I see him there, with his streaming hair
   And his eyes
Piercing beyond our human firmament,
Lit with a burning deathless discontent.

1917

THE VETERAN

He stumbles silver-haired among his bees,
Now with the warm sun mantling him; he plods
Taking his honey under the pippin-trees,
Where every sprig with rich red harvest nods.
   He marks the skies' intents,
And like a child, his joy still springing new,
In this fantastic garden the year through
He steeps himself in nature's opulence,

Mellow between the leafy maze smiles down
September's sun, swelling his multitude
Of gold and red and green and russet-brown
Lavished in plenty's lusty-handed mood
   For this old man who goes
Reckoning ripeness, shoring the lolling sprays,
And fruits which early gusts made castaways—
From the deep grasses thriftily rescuing those.

Babble he will, lingeringly, lovingly,
Of all the glories of this fruitful place,
Counting the virtues of each several tree,
Her years, her yield, her hardihood or grace;
   While through this triumph-song,
As through their shielding leaves, the year's fruits burn
In bright eye-cozening colour, turn by turn,
From cool black cherries till gold quinces throng

Blossoming the blue mists with their queenly scent.
Who hearing him can think what dragging years
Of drouthy raids and frontier-fights he spent,
With drum and fife to drown his clamouring fears?
   Here where the grapes turn red
On the red walls, and honey in the hives
Is like drift snow, contentment only thrives,
And the long misery of the Line is dead.

Resting in his old oaken-raftered room,
He sits and watches the departing light
Crimsoning like his apple-trees in bloom,
With dreaming gratitude and calm delight.
   And fast the peering sun
Has lit the blue delft ranged along the wall,
The painted clock and Squirrel's Funeral,
And through the cobwebs traced his rusty gun.

And then the dusk, and sleep, and while he sleeps,
Apple-scent floods and honey's fragrance there,
And old-time wines, whose secret he still keeps,
Are beautiful upon the marvelling air.
   And if sleep seem unsound,
And set old bugles pealing through the dark,
Waked on the instant, he but wakes to hark
His bellman cockerel crying the first round.

1919

How bright a dove's wing shows against the sky
When thunder's blackening up in monstrous cloud;
How silver clear against war's hue and cry
Each syllable of peace the gods allowed!
Even common things in anguish have grown rare
As legends of a richer life gone by,
Like flowers that in their time were no one's care,
But blooming late are loved and grudged to die.

What mercy is it I should live and move,
If haunted ever by war's agony?
Nature is love and will remember love,
And kindly uses those whom fear set free.
Let me not even think of you as dead,
O never dead! you live, your old songs yet
Pass me each day, your faith still routs my dread,
Your past and future are my parapet.

You looked before and after! these calm shires,
The doting sun, the orchards all aflame,
These joyful flocking swallows round the spires,
Bonfires and turreted stacks—well may you claim,
Still seeing these sweet familiar bygones, all!
Still dwells in you their has-been, their to-be,
And walking in their light you fear no fall.
This is your holding: mine, across the sea,

Where much I find to trace old friendship by:
" Here one bade us farewell," " Here supped we then,"
" Wit never sweeter fell than that July "—
Even sometimes comes the praise of better men.
The land lies like a jewel in the mind,

And featured sharp shall lie when other fades,
And through its veins the eternal memories wind
As that lost column down its colonnades.

Flat parcelled fields the scanty paths scored through,
Woods where no guns thrust their lean muzzles out,
Small smoky inns, we laughed at war's ado!
And clutching death, to hear, fell into doubt.
Christ at each crossroad hung, rich belfries tolling,
Old folks a-digging, weathercocks turned torches,
Half-hearted railways, flimsy millsails rolling—
Not one, but by the host for ever marches.

SHEPHERD

Evening has brought the glow-worm to the green,
And early stars to heaven, and joy to men;
The sun is gone, the shepherd leaves the pen
And hobbles home, while we for leisure lean
On garden pales. O shepherd old and kind,
Sweet may your musings and your slumbers prove!—
Where the rude chairs, of untanned osiers wove,
Creak to the dead of night, his rest he'll find:
And at his feet well pleased his dog will doze,
And not a traveller passes but he knows.

A country god to every childish eye—
Who sees the shepherd save when he comes home,
With untrimmed staff, smock stitched like honeycomb,
With great-tongued boots, and buskins to the thigh?
A seer, a country god—so thought conceives
His oracles of seasons foul or fair,
His weather-bitten looks, the wild white hair
That on his shoulders thatches like an eaves:

And he himself, proud of his antique toil,
Gossips with none that might such honour soil.

Sleep comes upon the village, the rich bee
From honeyed bells of balsams high is gone;
The windows palely shine; the owls whoop on,
But bats have slunk into their hollow tree.
The shepherd hours before has closed his eyes,
But he unseen will take his staff in hand
And walk to wake the morning through the land
Before the cockerel counts it time to rise.
High on the hill he dares the mist and dew
And sings before a sunbeam ventures through.

Now when the morning ripens and unfolds
Like beds of flowers the glories of the plain,
His heart leaps up at every steeple vane
And barn and kiln and windmill on the wolds;
For boyhood knew them all, and not a brook
But he has bathed and played the miller there;
By every green he's hurried to the fair
And tended sheep in every whitethorn nook.
Thus dreaming does he hurdle up the pen
And thinks how soon comes clipping-time agen.

His sheep his children are, each one he knows,
And well might know, who lay through winter storm
In cramping hulks with bracken scarce kept warm
While each one came from the poor frightened yoes.
He never bids or wants for holiday,
His sheep his children are and his delight:
That shepherds'-harvest makes the May so bright
When round his feet the lambs so frisk and play
And nuzzle in his sleeve and twitch his hand—
The prettiest dears, he calls them, in the land.

But May when music grows on every tree
Too quickly passes, shepherd's-roses die—
New dipt and shorn, they still delight the eye:
How fast they gather to his " Cub-buree "!
Even crows and jackdaws scrambling for the beans
Among the troughs are of his rustic clan,
Confess him king of bird and sheep and man;
And where he breaks his bread the emmet gleans.
The sun gives him old wisdom, the wind sings
Clear to his sense, his heart many hard things.

The stubble browsing comes, and from the grave
Autumn in half-hue swathes the rolling weald,
The blue smoke curls with mocking stealth afield,
And far-off lights, like wild eyes in a cave,
Stare at the shepherd on the bleaching grounds.
Deeply he broods on the dark tide of change,
And starts when echo sharp and sly and strange
To his gap-stopping from the sear wood sounds.
His very sheep-bells seem to bode him ill
And starling-whirlwinds strike his bosom chill.

Then whispering all his eighty years draw nigh,
And mutter like an Advent wind, and grieve
At perished summer, bidding him take leave
Of labour, take some comfort ere he die.
The hounded leaf has found a tongue to warn
How fierce the fang of winter, the lead rain
Brings him old pictures of the drowning plain,
When even his dog sulks loath to face the morn.
The sun drops cold in a watery cloud, the briars
Like starved arms still snatch at his withered fires.

But shepherd goes to warm him in his chair,
While in the blaze his dog growls at his dreams,
And on the hearth the leaping firelight gleams
That makes him think of one with ruddy hair

Who kept the sheep in ancient Bethlehem.
With trusting tears he takes his Bible, reads
Once more of still green banks and glittering meads
Where storms grow not, nor ever floods to stem;
Where the kind shepherd never takes them wrong,
And gently leads the yoes that are with young.

FOREFATHERS

Here they went with smock and crook,
    Toiled in the sun, lolled in the shade,
Here they mudded out the brook
    And here their hatchet cleared the glade:
Harvest-supper woke their wit,
Huntsman's moon their wooings lit.

From this church they led their brides,
    From this church themselves were led
Shoulder-high; on these waysides
    Sat to take their beer and bread.
Names are gone—what men they were
These their cottages declare.

Names are vanished, save the few
    In the old brown Bible scrawled;
These were men of pith and thew,
    Whom the city never called;
Scarce could read or hold a quill,
Built the barn, the forge, the mill.

On the green they watched their sons
    Playing till too dark to see,
As their fathers watched them once,
    As my father once watched me;

While the bat and beetle flew
On the warm air webbed with dew.

Unrecorded, unrenowned,
    Men from whom my ways begin,
Here I know you by your ground
    But I know you not within—
There is silence, there survives
Not a moment of your lives.

Like the bee that now is blown
    Honey-heavy on my hand,
From his toppling tansy-throne
    In the green tempestuous land—
I'm in clover now, nor know
Who made honey long ago.

GLEANING

Along the baulk the grasses drenched in dews
Soak through the morning gleaners' clumsy shoes,
And cloying cobwebs trammel their brown cheeks
While from the shouldering sun the dew-fog reeks.
Now soon begun, on ground where yesterday
The rakers' warning-sheaf forbade their way,
Hard clacking dames in great white hoods make haste
To cram their lapbags with the barley waste,
Scrambling as if a thousand were but one,
Careless of stabbing thistles. Now the sun
Gulps up the dew and dries the stubs, and scores
Of tiny people trundle out of doors
Among the stiff stalks, where the scratched hands ply—
Red ants and blackamoors and such as fly;

Tunbellied, too, with legs a finger long,
The spider harvestman; the churlish strong
Black scorpion, prickled earwig, and that mite
Who shuts up like a leaden shot in fright
And lies for dead. And still before the rout
The young rats and the fieldmice whisk about
And from the trod whisp out the leveret darts,
Bawled at by boys that pass with blundering carts
Top-heavy to the red-tiled barns.—And still
The children feed their corn-sacks with good will,
And farmwives ever faster stoop and flounce.
The hawk drops down a plummet's speed to pounce
The nibbling mouse or resting lark away,
The lost mole tries to pierce the mattocked clay
In agony and terror of the sun.

The dinner hour and its grudged leisure won,
All sit below the pollards on the dykes,
Rasped with the twinge of creeping barley spikes.
Sweet beyond telling now the small beer goes
From the hooped hardwood bottles, the wasp knows,
And even hornets whizz from the eaten ash;
Then crusts are dropt and switches snatched to slash,
While safe in shadow of the apron thrown
Aside the bush which years before was grown
To snap the poacher's nets, the baby sleeps.

Now toil returns, in red-hot fluttering light,
And far afield the weary rabble creeps,
Oft happening blind wheat, black among the white,
That smutches where it touches quick as soot;—
Oft gaping where the landrail seems afoot,
Who with such magic throws his baffling speech
Far off he sounds when scarce beyond arm's reach.
The dogs are left to mind the morning's gain,
But squinting knaves can slouch to steal the grain.

Close to the farm the fields are gleaned agen,
Where the boy droves the turkey and white hen
To pick the shelled sweet corn, their hue and cry
Answers the gleaners' gabble; and sows trudge by
With little pigs to play and rootle there,
And all the fields are full of din and blare.

So steals the time past, so they glean and gloat;
The hobby-horse whirs round, the moth's dust coat
Blends with the stubble, scarlet soldiers fly
In airy pleasure; but the gleaners' eye
Sees little but their spoils, or robin-flower
Ever on tenterhooks to shun the shower,—
Their weather-prophet never known astray;
When he folds up, then towards the hedge glean they.
But now the dragon of the skies droops, pales,
And wandering in the wet grey western vales
Stumbles, and passes, and the gleaning's done.
The farmer with fat hares slung on his gun
Gives folks goodnight, as down the ruts they pull
The creaking two-wheeled handcarts bursting full,
And whimpering children cease their teazing squalls
While left alone the supping partridge calls—
Till all at home is stacked from mischief's way,
To thrash and dress the first wild windy day;
And each good wife crowns weariness with pride,
With such small winnings more than satisfied.

THE PASTURE POND

By the pasture pond alone
I'll call the landscape all my own,
Be the lord of all I see
From water-fly to topmost tree,

63

And on these riches gloat this day
Till the blue mist warns away.

Here's no malice that could wither
Joy's blown flower, nor dare come hither;
No hot hurry such as drives
Men through their unsolaced lives;
Here like bees I cannot fare
A span but find some honey there.

The small birds and great as well
In these trees and closes dwell,
No cause found to grudge or brawl,
For nature gives enough for all;
Crows don't care what starling delves
Among these mole-heaps like themselves.

You thrush that haunt the mellow ground
And run with those quick glances round,
You'll run and revel through my brain
For a blue moon befooling pain;
You elms so full of birds and song,
Wear green coats there the winter long.

From the meadows smooth and still,
Where the peewits feed their fill
And into swirling rings upfly
With white breasts dazzling on the eye,
To the pool itself I come
And like rapture am struck dumb:

For if fields and air are free
The water's double liberty,
Where milch cows dewlap-deep may wade
Or hernshaw ply his angling trade—
Else what but vision dares intrude
That many-peopled solitude?

The astonished clouds seem lingering here
For dragon-flies so whip and veer
And take the sun and turn to flame,
They'd make the fastest cloud seem lame,
Or breaths of wind that sometimes fly
And cut faint furrows and are by.

So well may I admire the pool
Where thistles with their caps of wool
(Whence those sly winds some flecks purloin)
Stand sentinels at every coign,
And sorrels rusty-red have banned
Each place the thistles left unmanned.

But passing through, an old ally,
Into the bright deeps I may spy,
Where merry younkers, roach or rudd,
Jump for the fly and flounce and scud;
That care for no one now, and live
For every pleasure pools can give.

In russet weeds, by the sunken boat,
That spare each other room to float,
They hide along, grown fine and fat;
I hear them like a lapping cat
Feed from the stems till hunger's done—
Then out afresh to find the sun.

The moorhen, too, as proud as they,
With jerking neck is making way
In horse-shoe creeks where old pike rest
And beetles skate in jostling jest;
And overhead as large as wrens
Dance hobby-horses of the fens—

From all these happy folk I find
Life's radiance kindle in my mind,
And even when homeward last I turn
How bright the hawthorn berries burn,
How steady in the old elm still
The great woodpecker strikes his bill;

Whose labour oft in vain is given,
Yet never he upbraids high heaven;
Such trust is his. O I have heard
No sweeter from a singing bird
Than his tap-tapping there this day,
That said what words will never say.

But bells from humble steeples call,
Nor will I be the last of all
To pass between the ringers strong
And as of old make evensong;
While over pond and plat and hall
The first of sleep begins to fall.

Time, like an ever-rolling stream!
Through the yew the sun's last gleam
Lights into a glory extreme
The squirrel-carven pews that dream
Of my fathers far beyond
Their solitary pasture-pond.

NOVEMBER MORNING

From the night storm sad wakes the winter day
With sobbings round the yew, and far-off surge
Of broadcast rain; the old house cries dismay,
And rising floods gleam silver on the verge

Of sackclothed skies and cold unfruited grounds.
On the black hop-pole beats the weazen bine,
The rooks with terror's tumult take their rounds,
Under the eaves the chattering sparrows pine.

Waked by the bald light from his bed of straw,
The beggar shudders out to steal and gnaw
Sheep's locusts: leaves the last of many homes—
Where mouldered apples and black shoddy lie,
Hop-shovels spluttered, wickered flasks flung by,
And sharded pots and rusty curry-combs.

HIGH SUMMER

Now all the birds are flown, the first, the second brood,
Save those poor nestlings prisoned in cages for good;
The year seems to droop with its own midsummer might:
Tarnishing mosses crowd even runnels out of sight.

The ponds so wasted down scarce give their tenants breath,
Who plunge their heads to the ooze, and sicken to their
    death
Unless the clouds come on—already their dead float
Gleamless among the brambles that hide the moorhen's
    boat.

Slow walks the farmer's cob with ever-switching tail
Where the white dust-track glares; and labour dips his pail
But slow where the sand-vein still bubbles its clear spring;
The mat-mender squatting near wearily braids his string,

And curses at the thunder-flies that blacken on his arm
(As now they irk and terrify the gangers on the farm);
And thinks once again when he charged across the sand
In such torment, his reward—a hook for a hand;

And yet he labours on, till one o'clock drones,
Muttering how the flies make the flesh creep on his bones—
Then hobbles for his beer, and lively by and by
Talks forgotten battles with a tear in his eye.

EVENING MYSTERY

Now ragged clouds in the west are heaping,
All the hedges fall a-weeping,
   And in a thin green distance flowers
   The moon, the anemone of lonely hours.

The moon sheds diamonds on a myriad meadows
And her rays wander among wood shadows;
   Ere the last of sunset's flown
   She has made a new world of her own.

Old farm-houses with their white faces
Fly, and their ghosts have taken their places;
   Even the signposts like grim liars
   Point to trapping brakes and briars.

Tired birds roosting are not yet sleeping,
But stir and mutter at the wild eyes peeping;
   And sheep will not let silence lie,
   But blare about the hilltop sky

As though long-plotting dogs had broken
From kennel-chains, by the ringleader spoken,
   To harry the ewes in the light of the moon—
   The blood on their jaws will hang 'em anon.

But no, for miles the sheepfolds moan,
And dogs bay from their farms alone;
   Can she who shines so calm be fear?
   What poison pours she in slumber's ear?

SHEET LIGHTNING

When on the green the rag-tag game had stopt
And red the lights through alehouse curtains glowed,
The clambering brake drove out and took the road.
Then on the stern moors all the babble dropt
Among our merry men, who felt the dew
Sweet to the soul and saw the southern blue
Thronged with heat lightning miles and miles abroad,
Working and whickering, snakish, winged and clawed,
Or like old carp lazily rising and shouldering.
Long the slate cloud flank shook with the death-white
    smouldering:
Yet not a voice.
          The night drooped oven-hot;
Then where the turnpike pierced the black wood plot,
Tongues wagged again and each man felt the grim
Destiny of the hour speaking through him,
And then tales came of dwarfs on Starling Hill
And those young swimmers drowned at the roller mill,
Where on the drowsiest noon an undertow
Famishing for life boiled like a pot below:
And how two higglers at the Walnut Tree
Had curst the Lord in thunderstorm and He
Had struck them dead as soot with lightning then—
Which left the tankards whole, to take the men.

Many a lad and many a lass was named
Who once stept bold and proud; but death had tamed
The revel on the eve of May; cut short
The primrosing and promise of good sport,
Shut up the score book, laid the bright scarf by.

Such bodings mustered from the fevered sky;
But now the spring well through the honeycomb
Of scored stone rumbling tokened them near home:
The whip-lash clacked, the jog-trot sharpened, all
Sang Farmer's Boy as loud as they could bawl, ·
And at the Walnut Tree the homeward brake
Stopt for hoarse ribaldry to brag and slake.

The weary wildfire faded from the dark;
While this one damned the parson, that the clerk;
And anger's balefire forked from the unbared blade
At word of things gone wrong or stakes not paid:
The waiting driver stooped with oath to find
A young jack rabbit in the roadway, blind
Or dazzled by the lamps, as stiff as steel
With fear. Joe beat its brain out on the wheel.

CLOUDY JUNE

Above the hedge the spearman thistle towers
And thinks himself the god of all he sees;
But nettles jostle fearless where he glowers,
Like old and stained and sullen tapestries;
And elbowing hemlocks almost turn to trees,
Proud as the sweetbriar with her bubble flowers,
    Where puft green spider cowers
    To trap the toiling bees.

Here joy shall muse what melancholy tells,
And melancholy smile because of joy,
Whether the poppy breathe arabian spells
To make them friends, or whistling gipsy-boy
Sound them a truce that nothing comes to cloy.

No sunray burns through this slow cloud, nor swells
  Noise save the browsing-bells,
  Half sorrow and half joy.

Night comes; from fens where blind grey castles frown
A veiled moon ventures on the cavernous sky.
No stir, no tassel-tremble on the down:
Mood dims to nothing: atom-like I lie
Where nightjars burr and barking fox steps by
And hedgehogs talk and play in glimmering brown;
  Passions in such night drown,
  Nor tell me I am I.

MOLE CATCHER

With coat like any mole's, as soft and black,
And hazel bows bundled beneath his arm,
With long-helved spade and rush bag on his back,
The trapper plods alone about the farm:
And spies new mounds in the ripe pasture-land,
And where the lob-worms writhe up in alarm
And easy sinks the spade, he takes his stand
Knowing the moles' dark highroad runs below:
Then sharp and square he chops the turf, and day
Gloats on the opened turnpike through the clay.

Out from his wallet hurry pin and prong,
And trap, and noose to tie it to the brow;
And then his grand arcanum, oily and strong,
Found out by his forefather years ago
To scent the peg and witch the moles along.
The bow is earthed and arched ready to shoot

71

And snatch the death-knot fast round the first mole
Who comes and snuffs well pleased and tries to root
Past the sly nose peg; back again is put
The mould, and death left smirking in the hole.
The old man goes and tallies all his snares
And finds the prisoners there and takes his toll.

And moles to him are only moles; but hares
See him afield and scarcely cease to nip
Their dinners, for he harms not them; he spares
The drowning fly that of his ale would sip
And throws the ant the crumbs of comradeship.
And every time he comes into his yard
Grey linnet knows he brings the groundsel sheaf,
And clatters round the cage to be unbarred,
And on his finger whistles twice as hard.—
What his old vicar says, is his belief,
In the side pew he sits and hears the truth;
And never misses once to ring his bell
On Sundays night and morn, nor once since youth
Has heard the chimes afield, but has heard tell
There's not a peal in England sounds so well.

THE SCYTHE STRUCK BY LIGHTNING

A thick hot haze had choked the valley grounds
Long since, the dogday sun had gone his rounds
Like a dull coal half lit with sulky heat;
And leas were iron, ponds were clay, fierce beat
The blackening flies round moody cattle's eyes.
Wasps on the mudbanks seemed a hornet's size
That on the dead roach battened. The plough's increase
Stood under a curse.

Behold, the far release!
Old wisdom breathless at her cottage door
" Sounds of abundance " mused, hearing the roar
Of marshalled armies in the silent air,
And thought Elisha stood beside her there,
And loudly forecast ere the next nightfall
She'd turn the looking-glasses to the wall.

Faster than armies out of the burnt void
The hourglass clouds innumerably deployed,
And when the hay-folks next look up, the sky
Sags black above them; scarce is time to fly.
And most run for their cottages; but Ward,
The mower, for the inn beside the ford,
And slow strides he with shouldered scythe still bare,
While to the coverts leaps the great-eyed hare.

As he came in the dust snatched up and whirled
Hung high, and like a bell-rope whipped and twirled;
The brazen light glared round, the haze resolved
Into demoniac shapes bulged and convolved.
Well might poor ewes afar make bleatings wild,
Though this old trusting mower sat and smiled;
For from the hush of many days the land
Had waked itself: and now on every hand
Shrill swift alarm-notes, cries and counter-cries,
Lowings and crowings came and throbbing sighs.
Now atom lightning brandished on the moor,
Then out of sullen drumming came the roar
Of thunder joining battle east and west:
In hedge and orchard small birds durst not rest,
Flittering like dead leaves and like wisps of straws,
And the cuckoo called again, for without pause
Oncoming voices in the vortex burred.
The storm came toppling like a wave, and blurred

73

In grey the trees that like black steeples towered.
The sun's last yellow died. Then who but cowered?
Down ruddying darkness floods the hideous flash,
And pole to pole the cataract whirlwinds clash.

Alone within the tavern parlour still
Sat the grey mower, pondering Nature's will,
And flinching not to flame or bolt, that swooped
With a great hissing rain till terror drooped
In weariness: and then there came a roar
Ten-thousand-fold, he saw not, was no more—
But life bursts on him once again, and blood
Beats droning round, and light comes in a flood.

He stares and sees the sashes battered awry,
The wainscot shivered, the crocks shattered, and nigh,
His twisted scythe, melted by its fierce foe,
Whose Parthian shot struck down the chimney. Slow
Old Ward lays hand to his old working-friend,
And thanking God Whose mercy did defend
His servant, yet must drop a tear or two,
Adrift on times when that old scythe was new;
And stands in silent grief, nor hears the voices
Of many a bird that through the land rejoices,
Nor sees through the smashed panes the seagreen sky,
That ripens into blue, nor knows the storm is by.

THE POOR MAN'S PIG

Already fallen plum-bloom stars the green,
   And apple-boughs as knarred as old toads' backs
Wear their small roses ere a rose is seen;
   The building thrush watches old Job who stacks

74

The fresh-peeled osiers on the sunny fence,
  The pent sow grunts to hear him stumping by,
And tries to push the bolt and scamper thence,
  But her ringed snout still keeps her to the sty.

Then out he lets her run; away she snorts
  In bundling gallop for the cottage door,
With hungry hubbub begging crusts and orts,
  Then like the whirlwind bumping round once more;
Nuzzling the dog, making the pullets run,
And sulky as a child when her play's done.

THE COVERT

I always thought to find my love
  In some grove's ancient lair
Where though all day my steps might rove
  No one beside would fare:

Among the small forgotten woods
  With clambering ivy laden,
By ridings lost in bramble hoods
  I haunted for my maiden.

The greenest places I could find,
  Where underwoods are free
To flourish like the taller kind,
  Seemed homes where she might be.

And nothing but the loitering brook
  Or bee with question rude
Notice of my intrusion took
  Or felt my solitude.

75

The brook's eye mirrored me and seemed
    With my own thoughts to shine,
The bee patrolling where I dreamed
    Grumbled for countersign.

" And are not maidens fair to see
    In every green and town?
Why go you wooing secretly
    Through paths none travel down?

Why stare you on the sunny grove
    Like pale ghosts on moonlight?
But madness there will find a love
    And then be shut from sight."

Daphne from Phoebus fled of old
    And grew into a tree,
And all the loves of heaven, I hold,
    On earth now prisoned be.

And it may be, from earth or air,
    My longing shall unsphere
Beauty that only Daphnes wear,
    And so I tarry here—

Is there no spell upon this gloom
    So radiant, cool and green,
As promises the sudden bloom
    Of the loveliest ever seen?

I know not how or when the One
    Shall come—long have I gazed—
But shining like the vital sun
    Till even the wood's amazed,

The flower of cool and flower of bright
  And flower of woman too,
In the green dusk a dazzling light
  Yet sweet as manna-dew:

Gliding into seen Form, where she
  A locked-up secret lay,
From tingling air, from sighing tree—
  This Love shall crown my day.

—Thus murmured to himself the boy
  Where all the spinneys ring
With as rich syllables of joy
  As ever hailed the spring.

THE WATERMILL

I'll rise at midnight and I'll rove
Up the hill and down the drove
  That leads to the old unnoticed mill,
And think of one I used to love:
There stooping to the hunching wall
  I'll stare into the rush of stars
Or bubbles that the waterfall
  Brings forth and breaks in ceaseless wars.

The shelving hills have made a fourm
Where the mill holdings shelter warm,
  And here I came with one I loved
To watch the seething millions swarm.
But long ago she grew a ghost
  Though walking with me every day;
Even when her beauty burned me most
  She to a spectre dimmed away—

Until though cheeks all morning-bright
And black eyes gleaming life's delight
    And singing voice dwelt in my sense,
Herself paled on my inward sight.
She grew one whom deep waters glassed.
    Then in dismay I hid from her,
And lone by talking brooks at last
    I found a Love still lovelier.

O lost in tortured days of France!
Yet still the moment comes like chance
    Born in the stirring midnight's sigh
Or in the wild wet sunset's glance:
And how I know not, but the stream
    Still sounds like vision's voice, and still
I watch with Love the bubbles gleam,
    I walk with Love beside the mill.

The heavens are thralled with cloud, yet grey,
Half-moonlight swims the field till day,
    The stubbled fields, the bleaching woods;
Even this bleak hour was stolen away
By this shy water falling low
    And calling low the whole night through
And calling back the long ago
    And richest world I ever knew.

The hop-kiln fingers cobweb-white
With discord dim turned left and right,
    And when the wind was south and small
The sea's far whisper drowsed the night,
Scarce more than mantling ivy's voice
    That in the tumbling water trailed.
Love's spirit called me to rejoice
    When she to nothingness had paled:

For Love the daffodils shone here
In grass the greenest of the year,
   Daffodils seemed the sunset lights
And silver birches budded clear:
And all from east to west there strode
   Great shafted clouds in argent air,
The shining chariot-wheels of God,
   And still Love's moment sees them there.

REUNION IN WAR

The windmill in his smock of white
   Stared from his little crest,
Like a slow smoke was the moonlight
   As I went like one possessed

Where the glebe path makes shortest way;
   The stammering wicket swung.
I passed amid the crosses grey
   Where opiate yew-boughs hung.

The bleached grass shuddered into sighs,
   The dogs that knew this moon
Far up were hurrying sheep, the cries
   Of hunting owls went on.

And I among the dead made haste
   And over flat vault stones
Set in the path unheeding paced
   Nor thought of those chill bones.

Thus to my sweetheart's cottage I,
   Who long had been away,
Turned as the traveller turns adry
   To brooks to moist his clay.

Her cottage stood like a dream, so clear
  And yet so dark; and now
I thought to find my more than dear
  And if she'd kept her vow.

Old house-dog from his barrel came
  Without a voice, and knew
And licked my hand; all seemed the same
  To the moonlight and the dew.

By the white damson then I took
  The tallest osier wand
And thrice upon her casement strook,
  And she, so fair, so fond,

Looked out, and saw in wild delight,
  And tiptoed down to me,
And cried in silent joy that night
  Beside the bullace tree.

O cruel time to take away,
  Or worse to bring agen;
Why slept not I in Flanders clay
  With all the murdered men?

For I had changed, or she had changed,
  Though true love both had been,
Even while we kissed we stood estranged
  With the ghosts of war between.

We had not met but a moment ere
  War baffled joy, and cried,
"Love's but a madness, a burnt flare;
  The shell's a madman's bride."

The cottage stood, poor stone and wood,
    Poorer than stone stood I;
Then from her kind arms moved in a mood
    As grey as the cereclothed sky.

The roosts were stirred, each little bird
    Called fearfully out for day;
The church clock with his dead voice whirred
    As if he bade me stay

To trace with foolish fingers all
    The letters on the stones
Where thick beneath the twitch roots crawl
    In dead men's envied bones.

A FARM NEAR ZILLEBEKE

Black clouds hide the moon, the amazement is gone;
The morning will come in weeping and rain;
The Line is all hushed—on a sudden anon
The fool bullets clack and guns mouth again.
I stood in the yard of a house that must die,
And still the black hame was stacked by the door,
And harness still hung there, and the dray waited by.

Black clouds hid the moon, tears blinded me more.

1916 SEEN FROM 1921

Tired with dull grief, grown old before my day,
I sit in solitude and only hear
Long silent laughters, murmurings of dismay,
The lost intensities of hope and fear;
In those old marshes yet the rifles lie,
On the thin breastwork flutter the grey rags,
The very books I read are there—and I
Dead as the men I loved, wait while life drags

Its wounded length from those sad streets of war
Into green places here, that were my own;
But now what once was mine is mine no more,
I seek such neighbours here and I find none.
With such strong gentleness and tireless will
Those ruined houses seared themselves in me,
Passionate I look for their dumb story still,
And the charred stub outspeaks the living tree.

I rise up at the singing of a bird
And scarcely knowing slink along the lane,
I dare not give a soul a look or word
Where all have homes and none's at home in vain:
Deep red the rose burned in the grim redoubt,
The self-sown wheat around was like a flood,
In the hot path the lizard lolled time out,
The saints in broken shrines were bright as blood.

Sweet Mary's shrine between the sycamores!
There we would go, my friend of friends and I,
And snatch long moments from the grudging wars,
Whose dark made light intense to see them by.

Shrewd bit the morning fog, the whining shots
Spun from the wrangling wire; then in warm swoon
The sun hushed all but the cool orchard plots,
We crept in the tall grass and slept till noon.

WAR AUTOBIOGRAPHY

WRITTEN IN ILLNESS

Heaven is clouded, mists of rain
Stream with idle motion by;
Like a tide the trees' refrain
Wearies me where pale I lie,
Thinking of sunny times that were
Even in shattered Festubert;
Stubborn joys that blossomed on
When the small golden god was gone

Who tiptoe on his spire surveyed
Yser north from Ypres creeping,
And, how many a sunset! made
A longed-for glory amid the weeping.
In how many a valley of death
Some trifling thing has given me breath,
And when the bat-like wings brushed by
What steady stars smiled in the sky!

War might make his worst grimace,
And still my mind in armour good
Turned aside in every place
And saw bright day through the black wood:
There the lyddite vapoured foul,
But there I got myself a rose;
By the shrapnelled lock I'd prowl
To see below the proud pike doze.

Like the first light ever streamed
New and lively past all telling,
When I dreamed of joy I dreamed,
The more opprest the more rebelling;
Trees ne'er shone so lusty green
As those in Hamel valley, eyes
Did never such right friendship mean
As his who loved my enterprise.

Thus the child was born again
In the youth, the toga's care
Flung aside—desired, found vain,
And sharp as ichor grew the air:
But the hours passed and evermore
Harsher screamed the condor war,
The last green tree was scourged to nothing,
The stream's decay left senses loathing,

The eyes that had been strength so long
Gone, or blind, or lapt in clay,
And war grown twenty times as strong
As when I held him first at bay;
Then down and down I sank from joy
To shrivelled age, though scarce a boy,
And knew for all my fear to die
That I with those lost friends should lie.

Now in slow imprisoned pain
Lie I in the garret bed,
With this crampt and weighted brain
That scarce has power to wish me fled
To burst the vault and soar away
Into the apocalypse of day,
And so regain that tingling light
That twice has passed before my sight.

Triumph! How strange, how strong had triumph come
On weary hate of foul and endless war
When from its grey gravecloths awoke anew
The summer day. Among the tumbled wreck
Of fascined lines and mounds the light was peering,
Half-smiling upon us, and our newfound pride;
The terror of the waiting night outlived,
The time too crowded for the heart to count
All the sharp cost in friends killed on the assault.
No hook of all the octopus had held us,
Here stood we trampling down the ancient tyrant.
So shouting dug we among the monstrous pits.

Amazing quiet fell upon the waste,
Quiet intolerable to those who felt
The hurrying batteries beyond the masking hills
For their new parley setting themselves in array
In crafty fourms unmapped.
                                        No, these, smiled faith,
Are dumb for the reason of their overthrow.
They moved not back, they lie among the crews
Twisted and choked, they'll never speak again.
Only the copse where once might stand a shrine
Still clacked and suddenly hissed its bullets by.
The War would end, the Line was on the move,
And at a bound the impassable was passed.
We lay and waited with extravagant joy.

Now dulls the day and chills; comes there no word
From those who swept through our new lines to flood
The lines beyond? but little comes, and so
Sure as a runner time himself's accosted.

And the slow moments shake their heavy heads,
And croak, "They're done, they'll none of them get
    through,
They're done, they've all died on the entanglements,
The wire stood up like an unplashed hedge and thorned
With giant spikes—and there they've paid the bill."

Then comes the black assurance, then the sky's
Mute misery lapses into trickling rain,
That wreathes and swims and soon shuts in our world.
And those distorted guns, that lay past use,
Why—miracles not over!—all a-firing!
The rain's no cloak from their sharp eyes. And you,
Poor signaller, you I passed by this emplacement,
You whom I warned, poor daredevil, waving your flags,
Amid this screeching I pass you again and shudder
At the lean green flies upon the red flash madding.
Runner, stand by a second. Your message.—He's gone,
Falls on a knee, and his right hand uplifted
Claws his last message from his ghostly enemy,
Turns stone-like. Well I liked him, that young runner,
But there's no time for that. O now for the word
To order us flash from these drowning roaring traps
And even hurl upon that snarling wire?
Why are our guns so impotent?

                                        The grey rain,
Steady as the sand in an hourglass on this day,
Where through the window the red lilac looks,
And all's so still, the chair's odd click is noise—
The rain is all heaven's answer, and with hearts
Past reckoning we are carried into night
And even sleep is nodding here and there.

The second night steals through the shrouding rain.
We in our numb thought crouching long have lost
The mockery triumph, and in every runner

86

Have urged the mind's eye see the triumph to come,
The sweet relief, the straggling out of hell
Into whatever burrows may be given
For life's recall. Then the fierce destiny speaks.
This was the calm, we shall look back for this.
The hour is come; come, move to the relief!
Dizzy we pass the mule-strewn track where once
The ploughman whistled as he loosed his team;
And where he turned home-hungry on the road,
The leaning pollard marks us hungrier turning,
We crawl to save the remnant who have torn
Back from the tentacled wire, those whom no shell
Has charred into black carcasses—Relief!
They grate their teeth until we take their room,
And through the churn of moonless night and mud
And flaming burst and sour gas we are huddled
Into the ditches where they bawl sense awake
And in a frenzy that none could reason calm,
(Whimpering some, and calling on the dead)
They turn away: as in a dream they find
Strength in their feet to bear back that strange whim
Their body.
                    At the noon of the dreadful day
Our trench and death's is on a sudden stormed
With huge and shattering salvoes, the clay dances
In founts of clods around the concrete sties,
Where still the brain devises some last armour
To live out the poor limbs.
                              This wrath's oncoming
Found four of us together in a pillbox,
Skirting the abyss of madness with light phrases,
White and blinking, in false smiles grimacing.
The demon grins to see the game, a moment
Passes, and—still the drum-tap dongs my brain
To a whirring void—through the great breach above me

The light comes in with icy shock and the rain
Horridly drops. Doctor, talk, talk! if dead
Or stunned I know not; the stinking powdered concrete,
The lyddite turns me sick—my hair's all full
Of this smashed concrete. O I'll drag you, friends,
Out of the sepulchre into the light of day,
For this is day, the pure and sacred day.
And while I squeak and gibber over you,
Look, from the wreck a score of field-mice nimble,
And tame and curious look about them; (these
Calmed me, on these depended my salvation).

There comes my sergeant, and by all the powers
The wire is holding to the right battalion,
And I can speak—but I myself first spoken
Hear a known voice now measured even to madness
Call me by name.
                    " For God's sake send and help us,
Here in a gunpit, all headquarters done for,
Forty or more, the nine-inch came right through,
All splashed with arms and legs, and I myself
The only one not killed not even wounded.
You'll send—God bless you! " The more monstrous fate
Shadows our own, the mind swoons doubly burdened,
Taught how for miles our anguish groans and bleeds,
A whole sweet countryside amuck with murder;
Each moment puffed into a year with death.
Still swept the rain, roared guns,
Still swooped into the swamps of flesh and blood,
All to the drabness of uncreation sunk,
And all thought dwindled to a moan, Relieve!
But who with what command can now relieve
The dead men from that chaos, or my soul?

THE CHILD'S GRAVE

I came to the churchyard where pretty Joy lies
  On a morning in April, a rare sunny day;
Such bloom rose around, and so many birds' cries,
  That I sang for delight as I followed the way.

I sang for delight in the ripening of spring,
  For dandelions even were suns come to earth;
Not a moment went by but a new lark took wing
  To wait on the season with melody's mirth.

Love-making birds were my mates all the road,
  And who would wish surer delight for the eye
Than to see pairing goldfinches gleaming abroad
  Or yellowhammers sunning on paling and sty?

And stocks in the almswomen's garden were blown
  With rich Easter roses each side of the door;
The lazy white owls in the glade cool and lone
  Paid calls on their cousins in the elm's chambered core.

This peace, then, and happiness thronged me around.
  Nor could I go burdened with grief, but made merry
Till I came to the gate of that overgrown ground
  Where scarce once a year sees the priest come to bury.

Over the mounds stood the nettles in pride,
  And, where no fine flowers, there kind weeds dared to
    wave;
It seemed but as yesterday she lay by my side,
  And now my dog ate of the grass on her grave.

He licked my hand wondering to see me muse so,
  And wished I would lead on the journey or home,
As though not a moment of spring were to go
  In brooding; but I stood, if her spirit might come

And tell me her life, since we left her that day
  In the white lilied coffin, and rained down our tears;
But the grave held no answer, though long I should stay;
  How strange that this clay should mingle with hers!

So I called my good dog, and went on my way;
  Joy's spirit shone then in each flower I went by,
And clear as the noon, in coppice and ley,
  Her sweet dawning smile and her violet eye!

THE LAST OF AUTUMN

From cloudy shapes of trees that cluster the hills
The calm blue morning into brightness climbs;
And joy unhoped-for holds us hushed, and grace
Lures love again to coigns whence the long vales
Lie beautiful; that to my watch-tower come
I haunt an hour, I warm to radiance too,
By oaks that seem to kindle with the dawn.
But near his noon the sun sheds dizzy light,
And burning boughs burn with the dawn of death.

Shorn empty fields! where yet the eye discerns
A harvest home; look how the expanses point
To what the crowded season scorned, to stubs
That hold afield their outlaw solitude,
The mandrakes of the farms; see grouping sheep
Dapple the broad pale green, nabbing or resting.

Haystacks and hurdles gleam for honour now
And troughs and hovels in the lonely spaces
Rejected once are headstones in each corner.

Now once again the heart that long had feasted
On revel of song and wing, then long had dimmed
Its airy pleasure, cannot let a bird
Chance by but counts him into memory's tribe.
For there the witty jay laughs; here on waves
Invisible ripples the linnet, gross rooks gabble,
Or pheasant in his gaudy coat clangs past.
These are the riches of our poverty,
And all is peopled, though so few are there.

When sometimes wells a springing music from
The belt of pines, then the glad moment cries
" The nightingale," nor that same little bird,
Who now in Abyssinia claps his wings,
Might grieve to own the clear recalling call.

Then, senses, quicken, for it is not long—
Though slowly flow the gentle shadows over.

Ivy with wasp and hornet buzzes still,
Blue glittering flies are sunning on the stones,
And the hives among the nettles' chalky flowers
Are toiling; welcome, wayside thistles' crown,
And rare-grown daisy in the meadow, shine,
Though your pale cheeks have lost their lovely red.

But the wind that frets the old and clinging leaves
Arises deep, the very dirge and knell
Of this doomed dream;
And sets the weasel, where she hangs and dries
To skin and bone, still with her whiskered snarl,
A-swaying on the barren sloe-tree's thorn.

For slow and sure comes change, and in the mass
Of time how swift! Look down the glade and know
The timber felled, the vast too-cumbrous branch
Fallen, by the pillar of white that lightning left.
The village grandsires knew another glade.
This day so seeming-still, so patient-paced
Will drop down precipice darkness to its grave,
The whirlpooled past, the legion roar of night
Rend the tired world and leave it to its winter:
Whose turbulent angers and fierce siege shall die
When newness comes to the birth.
                                    But who may tell
When spring shall be again? and if these eyes
Should then be shut to the brightness of her coming?
So for her phantom violets I'll not lose
These rich, these poor, these fading glowing lulls
Nor drown my joy in boding. Better it were
To be dull Thrift, than squander thus this day:
Dull Thrift, who now has sown his mite of land,
Has thrashed his corn and beans, and where the dew's
Quicksilver bubbles lodge and shine all day
In the cabbage leaves, and the last lady-bird
Wafts her bright rosy way, leans pencilling coombs
And cash upon his garden palisades.

OLD HOMES

O happiest village! how I turned to you
Beyond estranging years that cloaked my view
With all their wintriness of fear and strain;
I turned to you, I never turned in vain.
Through fields yet ringing sad with fancy's dirge,
Landscapes that hunt poor sleep to bedlam's verge,

Green grow your leas, and sweet resound your woods,
And laughing children paddle in your floods.

There the old houses where we lived abide,
And I shall see them, though hot tears should hide
The gaze of " home " from that which now I hold.
What though pulled down ?—to me they're as of old.
The garrets creak as I tiptoe the boards
To find the last lone tenant's fabled hoards,
And silver on the dun November sky
Through jarring panes I see the flood race by
Brown hop-hills where the black bines moulder out.
To these same panes, when full moon comes about,
I hastening home lift daring eyes to learn
If ghost eyes through their sullen crystal burn,
And feel what sight cannot report, and fall
A-shuddering even to face the unlit hall.

Passages crooked and slanted, ceilings stooped,
And yews with drowsy arras overdrooped
The windows of that home; the broad hearths wept
With every shower; adry the great vats slept,
Where one time kercher'd maids had toiled with a will:
Such nooks were here, a hundred scarce would fill.
And in the farm beside, the barn's sunk tiles
Enclosed a space like to the church's aisles.

Then all about these vasty walls our play
Would hold the evening's lanterned gloom at bay,
And senses young received each new-found thing
As meadows feel and glow with inbreathed spring:
Thence we have journeyed out to blue hills round,
The pilgrims of a day's enchanted ground,
And where we'd seen the crow or heron fly
Have made our chartless way, passed far inns by,

On edge of lily ponds have heard the jack
From unknown holes leap, and shrunk trembling back,
Have seen strange chimneys smoke, new runnels foam,
Until quite surfeited we turned for home,
Whose white walls rosy with the westering light
Still of our journey seemed the noblest sight.

Thence too when high wind through the black clouds'
    pouring,
Bowing the strong trees' creaking joints, went roaring,
Adventure was to splash through the sightless lane
When church-bells filled a pause of wind and rain,
And once within the venerable walls
To hear the elms without like waterfalls,
While the cold arches murmured every prayer,
And Advent hymns bade the round world prepare,
Prepare! The next day with pale seas amazed
We scarce had marvelled as we gaped and gazed
If this had been the tempest harbinger
Of the world's end and final Arbiter:
The pollards in the yellow torrent drowning,
The weir's huge jaw a-gnashing, all heaven frowning.

But there at length, beside that thunderous weir,
Our lot was cast, and no less generous here
Came each long day; not even the hours we spent
Under old Grammar's eye unkindly went.
We found his learning dry, in faith, and hit
Disaster in our sleights for leavening it;
But the big desks cut with heroic names,
The gilded panel trumpeting past fames,
Shields, pictures, solemn books of stars and sages,
Kindled our pride in sense of mightier ages,
That school had seen, and cannot see again.
Fair, fair befall her, though no urchin pen

Crawl through the summer hours beneath her beams.
Nor playground-haunters' shouts bestir her dreams;
Honoured among her aspens may she rise,
And her red walls long soothe the traveller's eyes.

Thence issued we among the scampering crew,
And crossed the green, and from the bridge down threw
Our dinner crumbs to waiting roach; or soft
Marauding climbed the cobwebbed apple-loft,
And the sweet smell of Blenheims lapped in straw
Made stolen pleasure seem a natural law;
Escape and plunder hurried us at last
To the weir-cottage where our lot was cast,
Poor as church mice, yet rich at every turn,
Who never guessed that man was made to mourn.

In this same country as the time fulfilled
When hops like ribbons on the maypole frilled
Their colonnaded props mile after mile,
And tattered armies gathered to the spoil,
We too invaded the green arbours ere
The day had glistened on earth's dewy hair,
And through the heat have picked and picked apace,
To fill our half-bin and not lose the race,
While our bin partner, fierce of eye and tongue,
Disliked our style and gave " when I was young."
And all about the clearing setts revealed
The curious colours of the folk afield,
The raven hair, the flamy silk, the blue
Washed purple with all weathers; crime's dark crew;
Babes at the breast; old sailors chewing quids;
And hyacinth eyes beneath soon-dropt eyelids.
The conquest sped, the bramlings, goldings small,
The heavy fuggles to the bins came all,
Garden past garden heard the measurer's horn
Blow truce—advance! until a chillier morn

95

Saw the last wain load up with pokes and go,
And an empty saddened field looked out below
On trees where smouldered the quick fever-tingé
Of Autumn, on the river's glaucous fringe,
And our own cottage, its far lattice twinkling
Across tired stubble sown with sheep-bells' tinkling.
On airy wings the warning spirit sighed,
But we, we heard not, thinking of Christmastide.

A love I had, as childhood ever will,
And our first meeting I'll remember still;
When to the farmhouse first we went, the may
With white and red lit hedgerows all the way,
And there I saw her, in a red-may cloak
To church going by; so delicately she spoke,
So gracefully stept, so innocent-gay was her look,
I got a flower; she put it in her book.
And after, many eves, we walked for hours
Like loving flowers among the other flowers,
And blushed for pride when other girls and boys
Laughed at us sweethearts in the playhour's noise—
No more, this was a silly simple thing;
Those two can never now walk so in spring;
But to look back to child with child's primrosing
Is all the sweetness of each spring's unclosing.

Vision on vision blooms; long may they bloom,
Through years that bring the philosophic gloom,
Sweetening sleep with its strange agonies racked,
And shedding dew on every parching tract,
In every pleasant place a virtue adding,
A herb of grace to keep the will from madding:
And, happiest village, still I turn to you,
The alabaster box of spikenard, you;
To your knoll trees, your slow canal return,
In your kind farms or cottages sojourn;

Enjoy the whim that on your church tower set
The lead cowl like a Turkish minaret;
Beat all your bounds, record each kiln and shed,
And watch the blue mists on each calm close spread.
My day still breaks beyond your poplared East
And in your pastoral still my life has rest.

COUNTRY SALE

Under the thin green sky, the twilight day,
The old home lies in public sad array,
Its time being come, the lots ranged out in rows,
And to each lot a ghost. The gathering grows
With every minute, neckcloths and gold pins;
Poverty's purples; red necks, horny skins,
Odd peeping eyes, thin lips and hooking chins.

Then for the skirmish, and the thrusting groups
Bidding for tubs and wire and chicken coops,
While yet the women hang apart and eye
Their friends and foes and reckon who will buy.
The noisy field scarce knows itself, not one
Takes notice of the old man's wavering moan
Who hobbles with his hand still brushing tears
And cries how this belonged here sixty years,
And picks his brother's picture from the mass
Of frames; and still from heap to heap folks pass.

The strife of tongues even tries the auctioneer,
Who, next the dealer smirking to his leer,
A jumped-up jerky cockerel on his box,
Runs all his rigs, cracks all his jokes and mocks;
" Madam, now never weary of well-doing,"
The heavy faces gleam to hear him crowing.

And swift the old home's fading. Here he bawls
The white four-poster, with its proud recalls,
But we on such old-fashioned lumber frown;
" Passing away at a florin," grins the clown.
Here Baskett's Prayer Book with his black and red
Finds no more smile of welcome than the bed,
Though policeman turn the page with wisdom's looks:
The hen-wives see no sense in such old books.
Here painted trees and well-feigned towers arise
And ships before the wind, that sixpence buys.

All's sold; then hasty vanmen pile and rope
Their loads, and ponies stumble up the slope
And all are gone, the trampled paddock's bare;
The children round the buildings run and blare,
Thinking what times these are! not knowing how
The heavy-handed fate has brought them low,
Till quartern loaf be gone too soon to-day,
And none is due to-morrow. Long, then, play,
And make the lofts re-echo through the eve,
And sweeten so the bitter taking-leave.

So runs the world away. Years hence shall find
The mother weeping to her lonely mind,
In some new place, thin set with makeshift gear,
For the home she had before the fatal year;
And still to this same anguish she'll recur,
Reckoning up her fine old furniture,
The tall clock with his church-bell time of day,
The mirror where so deep the image lay,
The china with its rivets numbered all,
Seeming to have them in her hands—poor soul,
Trembling and crying how these, loved so long,
So beautiful, all went for an old song.

WINTER: EAST ANGLIA

In a frosty sunset
  So fiery red with cold
The footballers' onset
  Rings out glad and bold;
Then boys from daily tether
  With famous dogs at heel
In starlight meet together
  And to farther hedges steal;
Where the rats are pattering
  In and out the stacks,
Owls with hatred chattering
  Swoop at the terriers' backs
And, frost forgot, the chase grows hot
  Till a rat's a foolish prize,
But the cornered weasel stands his ground,
Shrieks at the dogs and boys set round,
Shrieks as he knows they stand all round,
  And hard as winter dies.

THE CROWN INN

Round all its nooks and corners goes
  The evening talk, in this old inn;
The darkening room by use well knows
  Each thread of life that these upspin.

The triumphs of the wooer, player,
  Eclogues of praise for mead and beer,
The fabled wealth, the generous fair
  Ring round the wonted changes here.

99

In elmtrees' gloom the western ray
 Drowns, the sad cloud steals like a shroud
Drawn over one that died to-day,
 And to my spirit memory-bowed

The world with all its wars and wails
 Seems turning slow; but here are some
With whom no black gazette prevails,
 Whom no disaster renders dumb.

Against the thunderclouds of race
 Their cottage candles give them light,
They like their clocks keep one same pace
 While empires shudder into night.

THE MIDNIGHT SKATERS

The hop-poles stand in cones,
 The icy pond lurks under,
The pole-tops steeple to the thrones
 Of stars, sound gulfs of wonder;
But not the tallest there, 'tis said,
Could fathom to this pond's black bed.

Then is not death at watch
 Within those secret waters?
What wants he but to catch
 Earth's heedless sons and daughters?
With but a crystal parapet
Between, he has his engines set.

Then on, blood shouts, on, on,
 Twirl, wheel and whip above him,
Dance on this ball-floor thin and wan,
 Use him as though you love him;

Court him, elude him, reel and pass,
And let him hate you through the glass.

PRIDE OF THE VILLAGE

A new grave meets the hastiest passer's eye,
It's reared so high, it lacks not some white wreath;
Old ones are not so noticed; low they lie
And lower till the equal grass forgets
The bones beneath.
His now, a modest hillock it must be,
The wooden cross scarce tells such as pass by
The painted name; beneath the chestnut tree
Sleep centuries of such glories and regrets.

But I can tell you, boys who that way run
With bat and ball down to the calm smooth leas,
Your village story's somewhere bright with one
To whom all looked with an approving joy
In hours like these.
Cricket to us, like you, was more than play,
It was a worship in the summer sun,
And when Tom Fletcher in the month of May
Went to the field, the feet of many a boy

Scarce pressed the buttercups; then we stood there
Rapt, as he took the bat and lit day's close,
Gliding and glancing, guiding fine or square
The subtlest bowls, and smoothing, as wave-wise
Rough-hurled they rose,
With a sweet sureness; his especial ease
Did what huge sinews could not; to a hair
His grey eye measured, and from the far trees
Old watchers lobbed the ball with merry cries.

And when the whitened creases marked the match,
Though shaking hands and pipes gone out revealed
The hour's impress and burden, and the catch
Or stumps askew meant it was Tom's turn next,
He walked afield
Modest, and small, and seldom failed to raise
Our score and spirits, great delight to watch;
And where old souls broke chuckling forth in praise
Round the ale booth, Tom's cricket was the text.

Summers slipt out of sight; next summer—hush!
The winter came between, and Tom was ill,
And worse, and with the spring's sweet rosy flush,
His face was flushed with perilous rose; he stayed
Indoors, and still
We hoped; but elders said, "Tom's going home."
The brake took cricketers by inn and bush,
But Tom not there! What team could leave out Tom?
He took his last short walk, a trembling shade.

And "short and sweet," he said, for his tombstone
Would be the word; but paint and wood decay,
And since he died the wind of war has blown
His old companions far beyond the green
Where many a day
He made his poems out of bat and ball.
Some few may yet be left who all alone
Can tell you, boys who run at cricket's call,
What a low hillock by your path may mean.

MUFFLED

Black ponds and boughs of clay and sulky sedge
Make their dull answer to the inquiring eye;
With worrying weakness wrens flit through the hedge,
And black rooks blot the south's thin jaundice sky;
Black over heavy plough the lonely inn
Stares without message at the far black mill,
The dry leaves creep, one even dares to spin,
The sun's last wish dies ere it reach the hill.

With wrapt throat in the courtyard of the farm
Maid waits for maid; bells call them, arm-in-arm,
To Advent prayer; the half-lit church is waiting.
Emmanuel, come! now, parson, hail that light—
God knows we need one in this glum black night,
When even the owls and bats are hesitating.

THE PUZZLE

The cuckoo with a strong flute,
The orchard with a mild sigh,
Bird and blossom so salute
   The rainbow sky.

The brown herd in the green shade,
The parson in his lawn chair,
Poor and gentry both evade
   The furnace air.

The moon-inveigled mushroom
The crocus with her frail horn,
Gaze in dumb dread through the gloom
   Of late moist morn.

The dead leaf on the highlands,
The old tramp on the mill drove,
Each whirls on nor understands
God's freezing love.

NO CONTINUING CITY

The train with its smoke and its rattle went on,
And the heavy-cheeked porter wheeled off his mixed
    load;
She shivered, and stood as if loth to be gone,
Staring this way and that—on the watery road,
And the inn with its arbour all naked and bleak,
And the weir churning foam, and the meaningless oast;
Till her husband turned back, and he stroked her pale
    cheek.
" O dear," murmured she, " must we go? but at most
                    I shall never live here
                    Above half a year."

And he with eyes keen as his bright singing mind,
While the cab tumbled on through the drifts of brown
    mist,
Shared her trouble; but knew that his future designed
A loftier life, could they meantime exist:
Then he sparkled and rested, and kissed his young sweet,
And they turned to the village, and stopped at the green
To enter the schoolhouse with echoing feet;
And she scanned, and she planned, though she murmured
    between
                    " I can never stay here
                    Above half a year."

And now forty years of his scholars have passed,
Dunce, sluggard and prizeman; the master remains:
He has built a new wing; and the school cap's recast;
And he makes his old jokes about beauty and brains.
And *she* speaks of home, but it is not this place,
But where a white waterfall springs down the crags,
And she goes to the garret, and stares into space,
Yet smiles when he finds her. The village tongue wags,
                    "She'll never be here
                    At this time next year."

THE LAST RAY

Now the world grows weak again, the sinewed woods are
    all astrain,
And Tempest in his ecstasy on horn or pipe or harp or drum
Makes his mad symphony; he runs like wild hogs, stops
    like a child,
Shrieks like a warning water-bird, and mutters *fee* and *fo*
    and *fum*.

Now through all this travail fierce one sunbeam does not
    fail to pierce
The spider-curtained darkness in the attic of black Jacob's
    farm,
And finds up there the purple phial that waits this glance:
    the sun's espial
Is not alone: the poor soul there espies as well the lurking
    charm.

Gods, she cries, tiptoes and takes, and glaring opens, sniffs
    and shakes,
While on her soul the stormsong bursts, and groanings knell
    through roof and flue;

Clashing gloom is whirled across, she drinks, and smashes
the cold glass,
And sneers as one great laugh or gust huffs down the
writhing avenue.

AUGURY

What sweeter sight will ever charm the eye
Than robin come to claim his largess old,
And pinnacled against the eager sky
Daring the armies of the brazen cold?
And wren a-running, while the storm shrouds all
The swinging mill-sails and black ghosts of groves,
Among the weeds that shake beneath the wall—
She well may vie with him in all our loves.

The mystery of the dark birthday of spring
Ever to childhood flowered into a sign
As over me I saw the paired swans wing
In whose wild breasts the gods made the light shine;
And song and wing have measured year on year,
Recorders of my solitude, till the sun
Is the bright hymn of nations of the air,
And evening and the dream-like owl are one.

So copses green start out of time stol'n hence
Because they rang with nightingales above
Their fellows, so returns dear innocence
At recollection of the lulling dove.
For alms the redbreast comes, the wren dares run,
While rook and magpie saunter through the sky,
All with their kinship of the morning sun—
In what rare element they sing and fly!

But oh, how bitter burns these fair ones' pain
When satyr hands in cages shut their young,
The old ones coming with their food in vain
Till death's a mercy! Oh, how great the wrong
That shuts 'em in, that starves but one small owl
Snatched into glaring day and mocks his hate:
And who, the wonder is, but djinn and ghoul
Could steal one mothering wing for folly's bait?

HAWTHORN

Beneath that hawthorn shade the grass will hardly grow,
So many babes have played and kept the bare clay so,
So many loves delayed in the moonlight's ebb and flow—
    Daisy-chains and May beginnings,
    Fail not till I pass below.

The roots of this same thorn are polished like a stool,
Each grey and goblin horn grown craftwise beautiful,
And sometimes to adorn is left a tuft of wool—
    I envy still the merry runnings
    Of those that pass that way from school.

The moonlight through the may and the whisper fluttering
    there,
Like angels on their way to the lamp of pain and prayer,
Gleams and ripplings play, and we lay our forehead bare,
    For here the coolest, cleverest cunnings
    Know the unknown's wingèd air.

Come, little tiny child, here's white violets for thee,
Come, smiling beauty wild, love's the dryad of this tree,
And thou baptizèd mild, this thorny chapel see,
    And may I for all my sinnings
    Sit in this same sanctuary.

DEAD LETTERS

(T.L.H.)

There lay the letters of a hundred friends
Of one whose name and years—what else?—we knew;
   Unordered, faded, past and gone,
   Mere script that chance had let live on.

Now through this chaos of sad nothing-worth,
Of unknown moods and matters dead so long,
   We'll look, we said, for any trace
   Of those his friends whom years but grace.

And hurrying over pages thick as leaves
In Vallombrosa, now with surprised hush
   We met with Mary Shelley's name,
   Tumultuous for her dead Love's fame.

Nor without trembling could we lay our hand
To that remorseless parchment which recalled
   Poor Harriet staring on the cold
   Oblivious water, deathly bold.

How often, fine as this his silvered hair,
Appeared the charactery of Shelley's friend,
   That friend for whom the Ariel gay
   Went fleeting on a fatal day!

The face of Keats glowed out awhile, and Lamb
Seemed never far, the darling of our race;
   And here the tired heroic soul
   Of Landor lit a homely scroll;

And later names which England's genius bore,
Writ by the men, flashed out on our survey;
   And Muse and State we chose in pride
   From the great throng we cast aside.

We cast aside! poor relics, chill and dumb,
That told us nothing, seemed the chaff that time
   With his great tempest might have hurled,
   And no grain lost, from this wide world.

But scanning here more closely, at the last
We found our thoughts in these unknowns drawn down
   To comprehend the hopes and fears,
   The wrongs and harms that loosed these tears;

The half-starved fingers at their drudgeries,
The brain in fever and endeavouring still,
   The unechoed songs in beauty's praise,
   The affection urged in darkest days;

And more and more these nameless annals clutched
The hasty hand, the heart, till a hundred ghosts
   Of men unlauded, past and gone,
   Seemed friends that we had always known.

THAMES GULLS

   Beautiful it is to see
On London Bridge the bold-eyed seabirds wheel,
And hear them cry, and all for a light-flung crust
Fling us their wealth, their freedom, speed and gleam.
   And beautiful to see
Them that pass by lured by these birds to stay,

And smile and say "how tame they are"—how tame!
Friendly as stars to steersmen in mid seas,
And as remote as midnight's darling stars,
Pleasant as voices heard from days long done,
As nigh the hand as windflowers in the woods,
And inaccessible as Dido's phantom.

MASKS OF TIME

Then the Lark, his singing on a sudden done,
Fell through crystal sunrays to his twilight bed;
Then the woods as sharp and carved as Parthenon
Stood before charmed eyes for ever; time was dead.

Now is haste returned; the striding fury flings
That mad mantle abroad, and foots both Pole and path.
Swarming grasses hiss: pursue wild beaks and wings;
The clods roll their brown heads, all Golgotha in wrath.

ACHRONOS

The trunks of trees which I knew glorious green,
Which I saw felled last year, already show
Rust-red their rounds; the twisting path between
Takes its new way already plain as though
It went this way since years and years ago.
The plough I saw my friend so often guide,
Snapped on the sly snag at the spinney side,
Lies rusting there where brambles overflow;
As gulfed in limbo lake as buried coins,
Which, once both bread and wine, now nothing mean.

The spider dates it not but spins in the heat,
For what's time past? but present time is sweet.
Think, in that churchyard lies fruit of our loins—
The child who bright as pearl shone into breath
With the Egyptian's first-born shares coeval death.

HARVEST

So there's my year, the twelvemonth duly told
Since last I climbed this brow and gloated round
Upon the lands heaped with their wheaten gold,
And now again they spread with wealth imbrowned—
    And thriftless I meanwhile,
What honeycombs have I to take, what sheaves to pile?

I see some shrivelled fruits upon my tree,
And gladly would self-kindness feign them sweet;
The bloom smelled heavenly, can these stragglers be
The fruit of that bright birth? and this wry wheat,
    Can this be from those spires
Which I, or fancy, saw leap to the spring sun's fires?

I peer, I count, but anxious is not rich,
My harvest is not come, the weeds run high;
Even poison-berries ramping from the ditch
Have stormed the undefended ridges by;
    What Michaelmas is mine!
The fields I thought to serve, for sturdier tillage pine.

But, hush—Earth's valleys sweet in leisure lie;
And I among them wandering up and down
Will taste their berries, like the bird or fly,
And of their gleanings make both feast and crown.
    The Sun's eye laughing looks.
And Earth accuses none that goes among her stooks.

STRANGE PERSPECTIVE

Happy the herd that in the heat of summer
Wades in the waters where the willows cool them,
From murmuring midday that singes the meadow,
And turns very tansies, fire-flowers, tindery.
Naked at noon there, naughtiness too wantons,
From bank bold jumping, and bough down dandling,
Of chimed hour chainless and churlish duty.
I see the glad set, who am far off sentenced;
Their lily limbs dazzle over long dry pastures;
And rude though ridges are risen between us,
Miles of mountains morosely upthrusting,
And dim and downward my gaze now droops,
My pool beyond pasture by a strange perspective
Is plain, and plunging its playmates gleam,
Hustling the staid herd into hazardous shadows.

RUE DU BOIS

Harmonious trees, whose lit and lissom graces
    For ever brighten on my hastening eye,
Calmed by whose leisure, by whose great griefs raptured,
    I cared not if the word were live or die,

Oh that I might with kisses and caresses
    Reveal that love to you, most lovely Powers,
And like the sun or trembling dew be welcome,
    And see no winter to our green amours!

This heart that glows at myriad-mantled beauty
    And at a gleam in voice or touch or eye
Is lost and lispering, dazzled and disastered,
    This heart the plaything of the Passing By—

O could it but be held by these wood-wonders,
  That time but gently, gently shine and sing!
Death first! and even in death this heart, dust-crumbled,
  Will never give an aspen to the spring.

TO JOY

Is not this enough for moan
To see this babe all motherless—
A babe beloved—thrust out alone
  Upon death's wilderness?
Our tears fall, fall, fall—I would weep
My blood away to make her warm,
Who never went on earth one step,
  Nor heard the breath of the storm.
How shall you go, my little child,
Alone on that most wintry wild?

A PSALM

O God, in whom my deepest being dwells,
Unasking what Thy form or mind may be,
Hear once again the sighing trust that wells
From my late wildered breast, and comfort me!
I call, I call from this long vale of tears,
I lift my eyes to the hills, there fancying Thee:
O Thou whose whim or wisdom shapes the spheres,
Yet be my temple and kind sanctuary!

The ages like an army without end
Go conquering on, and lay rich trophies by,
Their cities triumph and their fanes extend,
In their strong rooms the taken mysteries lie.

But thence does earth put on a lovelier hue?
Does their light hearten, or but terrify?
Fast cometh on my enemy anew,
And Bashan's arrows darken all the sky.

Thence as a bird, as that poor wood-pigeon
Which with shot wings from the curst gunner flees
Through the wild scowling evening on and on
And finds a mercy in some secret trees,
I fly to Thee; I lodge me in those boughs
Which shadowed through the hottest tyrannies
Thy early shepherds; then refreshed I rouse,
Spring through white skies, and light in flowering leas.

Reason, still mining in her rocks and reefs,
Is still refining; fancy paints as Thee
A witenagemot of dæmon chiefs
For ever vying; forces not to see.
But nothing better than my fathers, I
Hear rather the heart's summons and go free
From all the heartless claims that multiply,
And still Thee Father call, and come to Thee.

Then though the light of the age far off reveal
Some tragic theme, and doubt grow doubly strong,
I happy am; I dare and need to kneel
To One who tuned great David's life to song.
My prayer, no more than not to lose that dew
And dawn that failed not yet my path along:
O God that Abraham and our Vaughan knew,
Hide not Thyself, let first love prove not wrong.

THE DEATH-MASK OF JOHN CLARE

Kind was the hand that at the last
   This mortal likeness drew,
And more than kindness took the cast—
   'Twas prophecy, come true.

Doubt surely questioned, why record
   This old forgotten face?
But after-time with love's reward
   Has blessed the act of grace.

So, Clare, your rich, sweet, serious gaze
   Meets me through sixty years,
Now sets my wonderment ablaze,
   Now fascinates my tears.

I think when young you blushed among
   The gay town's curious eyes;
How tripped the truth from beauty's tongue,
   " A noble in disguise! "

God's noble, slave of earth, upraised
   To bright conception's song,
And by the world down dashed and dazed,
   How held you out so long?

For even the raven's young, you said,
   Are answered when they cry,
But when your children wanted bread,
   At length the stony sky

Seemed all one frown! the tired mind groaned
   Defeat day after day,
And purpose to the dust dethroned
   In riddles mocked the play.

Then from loved fields, from wife, from child,
　You helplessly were haled;
Where the thronged mad high heaven reviled
　Was freedom's friend enjailed.

Twenty dim years you lived where some
　Gnash ivy from the wall,
And others shrieking, others dumb
　With their dark dæmons brawl.

Still welcomed you the bee and bird
　In morning's crystal dew,
Still garlanded with spring-like word
　Spring's " gold yminted new."

A thrall, you reached the allotted span,
　Your countenance wore no sign
Of your Bastille, you looked the Man,
　Serene and nigh divine.

Came death; the boundary wall was cleft,
　Green pastures mile on mile
Gleamed flowers your childhood knew, you left
　Your prison with a smile.

INTIMATIONS OF MORTALITY

　　—I am only the phrase
　　Of an unknown musician;
　　By a gentle voice spoken
　　I stole forth and met you
　　In halcyon days.
Yet, frail as I am, you yourself shall be broken
Before we are parted; I have but one mission:
　　Till death to beset you.

—I am only the glowing
Of a dead afternoon,
When you, full of wonder,
Your hand in your mother's,
Up great streets were going.
Pale was my flame, and the cold sun fell under
The blue heights of houses; but I shall gleam on
In your life past all others.

—I am only the bloom
Of an apple-tree's roses,
That stooped to the grass
Where the robins were nesting
In an old vessel's womb.
Dead is the tree, and your steps may not pass
The place where it smiled; but I'll come, till death closes
My ghostly molesting.

—You phantoms, pursue me,
Be upon me, amaze me,
Though nigh all your presence
With sorrow enchant me,
In sorrow renew me!
Songless and gleamless I near no new pleasance,
In subtle returnings of ecstasy raise me,
To my winding-sheet haunt me!

A "FIRST IMPRESSION" (TOKYO)

No sooner was I come to this strange roof,
Beyond broad seas, half round the swaying world,
Than came the pretty ghost, the sudden sweet
And most sad spirit of my vanished child:
From the bare corners of the unknown room

She peeped with beauty's eyes, till my eyes rained
Their helpless tears once more; and there, and there
Was my dead baby baffling with dream presence,
And singing, till I thought I must be mad—
Was not all silent? yet, I heard her song.
Child, will not Orcus yield you? that small voice
Wafts, as I know, from where I cannot come,
And that smile glimmers like the ethereal flowers
In your far meadows: would that earth's kind flowers
Might now be golden in your toddling path!

Thus moved my musings, till at length I heard
From neighbouring doors slid back along their grooves
Small children scurrying, with the hastiest joy,
And quick young voices planning glorious play;
I looked, and saw some in their dresses bright
Laying themselves a garden in the dust,
With broad green leaves to be their noble trees,
With beds marked out, and buds desired to grow.
Oh, millions, millions in this world (I cried)
Are the glad children blossoming fast and fair,
Filling both homes and homeless hearts with airs
Of young eternity; and other worlds
Have their child millions too, so kind in this
Is nature; and though one of these dear blooms
Fall, still great childhood lords it all the way,
And the whole earth may see and hear and glory.

The children shouted as this way and that
They hurried, and I glittered with their light,
And loved them, as if kindred of my own,
And left glad faith in nature's motherhood.
To me, were not two younglings given and spared?
I saw them in the Suffolk lane; high flowed
The tide of love and surety in my breast.
But still, I saw a ghost, and lacked one child.

WARNING TO TROOPS

What soldier guessed that where the stream descended
In country dance beneath the colonnade
Of elms which cooled the halted troop, it played
Sly music, barely noted, never ended?
Or who, from war's concerns a moment missed,
At some church door turned white as came to him
One gold note struck by the hidden organist,
One note long-drawn through caverns cool and dim?

O marcher, hear. But when thy route and tramp
Pause by some falling stream, or holy door,
Be the deaf adder; bear not back to camp
That embryo music. Double not thy war.
Shun all such sweet prelusion. March, sing, roar,
Lest perilous silence gnaw thee evermore.

IN A COUNTRY CHURCHYARD

Earth is a quicksand; yon square tower
    Would still seem bold,
But its bleak flinty strength each hour
    Is losing hold.

Small sound of gasping undertow
    In this green bed!
Who shuts the gate will shut it slow,
    Here sleep the dead:

Here sleep, or slept; here, chance, they sleep,
    Though still this soil
As mad and clammed as shoals acreep
    Around them boil.

The earth slips down to the low brown
   Moss-eaten wall
Each year, and nettles and grasses drown
   Its crumbling crawl.

The dog-rose and ox-daisies on
   Time's tide come twirling,
And bubble and die where Joy is gone—
   Sleep well, my darling.

Seldom the sexton with shrewd grin
   Near thy grave-cloth,
With withered step and mumble thin
   Awakes eve's moth.

Not a farm boy dares here destroy,
   Through red-toothed nettles,
The chiff-chaff's nest, to strew the shells
   Like fallen petals.

The silver-hooded moth upsprings,
   The silver hour,
And wanders on with happy wings
   By the hush tower,

That reels and whirs, and never drops,
   That still is going;
For quicksand not an instant stops
   Its deadly flowing.

And is Joy up and dancing there
   Where deepening blue
Asks a new star? is that her hair
   There freshed with dew?

Here, O the skull of some small wretch,
   Some slaughtered jot,
And bones like bits of hated quitch
   Recount fate's plot.

So lies thy skull? This earth, even this
   Like quicksand weaves.
Sleep well, my darling, though I kiss
   Lime or dead leaves.

Sleep in the flux as on the breast,
   In the vortex loll;
In mid simoom, my innocence, rest;
   In lightning's soul

Bower thyself! But, joyous eyes,
   The deeps drag dull—
O morning smile and song, so lies
   Thy tiny skull?

BYROAD

Who knows not that sweet gloom in spring,
That waiting gloom, that grave delight
   In coming bloom,
   In the first flight
Of bird, or thought, so wild of wing?

Now when round hedgerow's earthy claws
And painted shells that blanch near by
   The dark grass swells
   And from the eye
In buds each old black nest withdraws,

I well might go to my old haunt
And find the green brook brushing down
    By celandine
    And sedges brown
And hoppers' houses grimed and gaunt.

I well might go where the burnt ring
And rusty kettles year on year
    Show life has yet
    Her freedoms dear—
And I will go, another spring.

It may be, I shall then unfold
Why with such thrill and venturous joy
    I crossed that rill,
    A hurrying boy,
One Lenten Sunday ages old.

The mild mysterious spring was there,
The silk palm glowed, the vole peeped shy
    Beside the road
    Where you and I
Went on and blest the orchard air.

Then coming to the timbered cot
Of your good friend, how deep it strook
    That he would lend
    His longed-for book,
Old Walton, which forthwith he got,

And by the window gave to me.
The apples in the window-sill,
    His humorous chin,
    I see them still;
I see his good wife getting tea.

But where's the mystery? There it was;
And is it there? And can I find
    Spring's dusk so fair
    Now that this mind
Looks far beyond such floating floss?

O look not out; the young spring broods
Too wondering-warm on nest and bough,
    Her dark eyes charm,
    Her babe leaps now,
And godhead glistens in those woods.

AN ANCIENT PATH

Rosy belief uplifts her spires
Anemone-frail in amaranth air
    That never hurts a thing:
This river's highway leads us there,
Hear how each crystal crispèd spring
Comes lightfoot down from shepherd shires,
Comes past the stones and roots and briars
    To journey with this king.
    And Honesty on his boat with bales
    And bags and barrels laded sails;
    The merry wind knows that white wing!
He sees those steeples, and he hails;
    And we'll go journeying there.
You must be by me, then be gone,
Then through the bush peep like a bird,
And then with arm in mine step on,
And like one in a legend sing,
    Or play with an angel word.
The silver bream jumps out of the stream,

Morn's diamonds ding from the blackbird's wing,
And through long glades that gilt wing speeds—
We'll go where this green river leads
And prismy light and bowing reeds
    To that sweet town,
With lilies lulled, to that sweet town
Whose airiest tiptoe chanticleer
Gleams on the west wind all the year;
Belief's our mark, we've crossed the down,
Time brought the eagle—now the dove!
And there's her sparkling belvedere—
    Come, my late and early love.

SOLUTIONS

The swallow flew like lightning over the green
And through the gate-bars (a hand's breadth between);
He hurled his blackness at that chink and won;
The problem scarcely rose and it was done.

The spider, chance-confronted with starvation,
Took up another airy situation;
His working legs, as it appeared to me,
Had mastered practical geometry.

The old dog dreaming in his frowsy cask
Enjoyed his rest and did not drop his task;
He knew the person of " no fixed abode,"
And challenged as he shuffled down the road.

These creatures which (Buffon and I agree)
Lag far behind the human faculty
Worked out the question set with satisfaction
And promptly took the necessary action.

By this successful sang-froid I, employed
On " Who wrote Shakespeare? " justly felt annoyed,
And seeing an evening primrose by the fence
Beheaded it for blooming insolence.

THE AGE OF HERBERT AND
VAUGHAN

Then it was faith and fairness,
    White sun and western wind,
When every moment spoke
    The Holy to the mind,
And quickened saints' awareness.

In close and pregnant symbol
    Each primrosed morning showed
The triune God's patrol
    On every country road,
In bushy den and dimble.

And where young Prue was sweeping,
    Or giggling at the gate,
Or Tom was scaring crows
    Or the dog Sam licked the plate
Or ewe and lamb were sleeping,

The witness still recorded
    Glance, phrase or incident
That appertained to Christ
    And by these shows was meant.
At once he stood rewarded!

THE WARTONS

Mild hearts! and modest as the evening bell
   That rings so often through your meadow rhyme,
May there be elms and belfries where you dwell,
   And the last streaks of day still gild old time!

In the new heaven and true Jerusalem
   Can such things be? That can they! where you rove
The glow-worm shall not hide his elvish gem,
   The owl with ghostly wing shall tour the grove.

And when the charms and fairies of the night
   Are changed to sparkling dew and morning's choir,
Gazing the vale farms, from some sheep-strown height,
   How will you welcome Phœbus' dancing fire!

On ancient arches shall your primrose peep,
   On diamond lattices your sunbeam play,
Across shy brooks your little peasants leap,
   And peace and innocence divide the day.

Nor shall the shades of poets not be seen
   Whom you have loved. Milton in his young prime,
Spenser and Chaucer on the daisied green
   Shall join with you and hear May-morning chime.

THE COMPLAINT

The village spoke: " You come again,
You left me for a world of men.
     Tell,
How you feel now my former spell? "

And I: " Sweet simpleton, old home—
Much charged, with puzzled heart I come;
   Still,
I think you are the nonpareil."

At that a breeze, a sigh was heard,
And thus the traveller caught the word,
   " Child,
Love's just and gentle; love you smiled;

But was it not my creed and dream
To fit you for a mightier theme?
   Proud
You stepped away to join the crowd.

And since, what hills, what skies you've known,
What streets of strength, what speaking stone!
   More,
The drama of terrestrial war;

And love the Atlantis, far and near,
And genius brightening sphere on sphere,
   Bounds
That only seemed thought's pleasure-grounds.

Thence come you with this accent dim,
With eyes that gaze till the tears brim?
   I . . .
But look, how small and poor I lie."

The sunny grass danced on the wall,
The smithy clanged, old Jesse Hall
   Flung
His jacket off, and scythed and sung;

From school the hungry youngsters rushed,
The caravan passed, the mill sluice gushed.
 " Dear,"
I answered, " all my ways led here."

AN INFANTRYMAN

Painfully writhed the few last weeds upon those houseless
  uplands,
    Cleft pods had dropt their blackened seeds into the
      trampled clay,
Wind and rain were running loose, and icy flew the whip-
  lash;
    Masked guns like autumn thunder drummed the outcast
      year away.

Hidden a hundred yards ahead with winter's blinding
  passion,
    The mule-beat track appeared half dead, even war's hot
      blood congealed;
The half-dug trenches brimmed like troughs, the camps lay
  slushed and empty,
    Unless those bitter whistlings proved Death's army in
      the field.

Over the captured ridge above the hurt battalion waited,
    And hardly had sense left to prove if ghost or living
      passed
From hole to hole with sunken eyes and slow ironic orders,
    While fiery fountains burst and clanged—and there
      your lot was cast.

Yet I saw your health and youth go brightening to the
  vortex,
    The ghosts on guard, the storm uncouth were then no
      match for you;
You smiled, you sang, your courage rang, and to this day
  I hear it,
    Sunny as a May-day dance, along that spectral avenue.

THE RESIGNATION

Live in that land, fair spirit and my friend,
Which you are wealthy in, where your estate
Ripples in wheat and sunshine without end,
And wood-rides never reach the glittering gate,
    Where fall the nymphal rills
    Down sunny hills;
    And shepherds there sit playing
    " Corinna's gone a-Maying "—
O ever may your rills like lovesongs run,
And each green height allure some shining One.

With that, your cities twinkle through warm miles
Of pastoral blue, and you at one thought move
Where blest bells chant and antique order smiles,
And love peeps down from airy nooks, your love.
    Her flowery lattice soon
    Beneath the moon
    May lodge the owl tu-whooing,
    For she'll have stolen a-wooing,
And where through dragon throats the spring leaps clear
Be whispering lest a wide-eyed rose should hear.

This was my country, and it may be yet,
But something flew between me and the sun;
The gnawed reeds blacken, the thinned poplars fret,
Leaves loll, would wake, and with a thrill are gone.
    The city faces stare
    Across the square
    When the burnt spire of vision
    Hangs in hurt indecision;
They guess strange menace where old safety throve,
That palest face among them was my love.

WOULD YOU RETURN?

Poppies never brighter shone, and never sweeter smelled
    the hay,
The town with its steeples looked made of silver all the
    way,
Down in the streamy valley like a treasure that town lay.

Who was not with me there? who in that crystal air
Hastened not beside me on the springy grass, did not stare
Miles ahead where those bright tops of mansioned hope
    were gems aflare?

Come then, know again this same knoll we paused upon,
These poplars with their flashing wind, this singing rill, this
    silent stone—
The sun pale peering at the shag-haired storm that swooped
    on Avalon!

AN ANNOTATION

The primrose way to th' everlasting bonfire.

MACBETH II, iii.

Like a puff'd and reckless libertine,
Himself the primrose path of dalliance treads.

HAMLET I, iii.

Emblem of early seeking, early finding,
Frailness whose patience stills the moody cries
Of old Time struggling through chaotic skies
Where the lashed sleet-gust foams, buffeting and blinding,
And then were ever the light in his calm eyes
May after May, a star so dear and mild
That love by the evening bell and you beguiled
Thinks echo charmed to your still bell replies;
Pilgrim, to whom the weaker sort will turn
Their pale looks, and your pale resolve responds,
Your paths are peace, they comfort and not burn,
There young Love strolls, old Adage stares in ponds.
With what strange wrong was Shakespeare mocked when he
So tossed you to the hooves of infamy?

ORNITHOPOLIS

Suggested by an Excellent Article, " Starlings in London," by
Mr. Eric Parker, " Spectator," March 6th, 1926

Not your least glory, many-gloried Wren,
Springs from these birds, that to your immense Dome
When eve grows glassy cold and clear, come home
   From fallow and blue fen;

Each flying to his mansion overhead,
The guest of genius, sure of man at last,
Though maelstrom roars and wild light volleys vast,
  Each calm and glad abed.

Never was convenant nor entente like this,
Which still shall gather confidence and joy;
Man's city chosen the birds' metropolis,
Whole myriads taken with a fair decoy!
Through tree and chimney-top the news is told,
With loud-tongued gossip of an age of gold.

ON THE PORTRAIT OF A COLONEL

G.H.H.

When now at this stern depth and shade of soul
I lift eyes to that most honoured face,
And yearn towards that harmony and whole
Of soldier creed and act and pride of place,
The eye's shrewd humour, the lip's generous grace,
The stirring zest, the power to make and give,
I feel my youth awake afresh and live,
And bugled morning glows and climbs apace.

Some stubborn clouds of conscience stain that prime,
And chilly creeps the muttering breeze, regret;
But still this picture kindles coming time,
And bids me gird myself for crossroads yet
Where through the inhuman tempestings of night
This man's commanding trust will be my sight.

DEPARTURE

The beech leaves caught in a moment gust
Run like bowled pennies in the autumn's dust
   And topple; frost like rain
Comes spangling down; through the prismy trees
Phœbus mistakes our horse for his,
   Such glory clothes his mane.

The stream makes his glen music alone
And plays upon shell and pot and stone—
   Our life's after-refrain;
Till in the sky the tower's old song
Reads us the hour, and reads it wrong,
And carter-like comes whistling along
   Our casual Anglian train.

LIBERTINE

In summer-time when haymaking's there
   And master fish leap out of the pools,
I'll take an oak for my easy chair,
   Be club and president, ruler and rules.

The dew of the dawn there haunts all day,
   The silver ripple and willow-wren chime;
The bee will pass on his gipsying way
   And everything dote on summer-time.

If sweet it is to be safe ashore
   When the merchantman plunges into the trough,
I think that ambush is sweetness galore
   Whence I may study, some furlongs off,

Old ale-faced industry mopping his brow,
  Hot shouldering and shaping heap on heap,
While I sit under the church-cool bough
  And a Dryad will peep when she thinks I'm asleep.

A HOUSE IN FESTUBERT

With blind eyes meeting the mist and moon
And yet with blossoming trees robed round,
With gashes black, nay, one great wound,
Amazing still it stands its ground;
  Sad soul, here stay you.

It held, one time, such happy hours,
Its tables shone with smiles and filled
The hungry—Home! 'twas theirs, is ours,
We house it here and laugh unkilled.
  Hoarse gun, now, pray you—

It knew the hand and voice of Sleep,
Sleep was its friend and nightly came,
And still the bony laths would keep
One friendship, but poor Sleep's gone lame.
  O poisoner, Mahu!

A hermit might have built a cell
Among those evergreens, beside
That mellow wall: they serve as well
For four lean guns. Soft, hermits, hide,
  Lest pride display you.

It hived the bird's call, the bee's hum,
The sunbeams crossing the garden's shade—
So fond of summer! still they come,
But steel-born bees, birds, beams invade.
  —Could summer betray you?

134

THE SENTRY'S MISTAKE

The chapel at the crossways bore no scar,
Nor near had whining covey of shells yet pounced,
The calm saints in the chapel knew no war,
No meaning there the horizon's roars announced;
   We halted, and were glad; the country lay
   After our marching like a sabbath day.

Round the still quadrangle of the great farm
The company soon had settled their new home;
The cherry-boughs were beckoning every arm,
The stream ran wrinkling by with playful foam,
   And when the guard was at the gateway set,
   Surrounding pastoral sweetly stole their wit.

So out upon the road, gamekeeper-like,
The cowman now turned warrior measured out
His up-and-down sans cursed bundook and spike,
Under his arm a cudgel brown and stout;
   An air of comfort and kind ownership,
   A philosophic smile upon his lip.

For it seemed sin to soil the harmonious air
With the parade of weapons built to kill.
But now a flagged car came ill-omened there.
The crimson-mottled monarch, shocked and shrill,
   Sent our poor sentry scampering for his gun,
   Made him once more " the terror of the Hun."

" There's something in the air," he said
   In the large parlour cool and bare;
The plain words in his hearer bred
   A tumult, yet in silence there
All waited; wryly gay, he left the phrase,
Ordered the march and bade us go our ways.

" We're going South, man "; as he spoke
   The howitzer with huge ping-bang
Racked the light hut; as thus he broke
   The death-news, bright the skylarks sang;
He took his riding-crop and humming went
Among the apple-trees all bloom and scent.

Now far withdraws the roaring night
   Which wrecked our flower after the first
Of those two voices; misty light
   Shrouds Thiepval Wood and all its worst:
But still " There's something in the air " I hear,
And still " We're going South, man," deadly near,

ILLUSIONS

Trenches in the moonlight, in the lulling moonlight
Have had their loveliness; when dancing dewy grasses
Caressed us passing along their earthly lanes;
When the crucifix hanging over was strangely illumined,
And one imagined music, one even heard the brave bird
In the sighing orchards flute above the weedy well.
There are such moments; forgive me that I note them,

Nor gloze that there comes soon the nemesis of beauty,
In the fluttering relics that at first glimmer wakened
Terror—the no-man's ditch suddenly forking:
There, the enemy's best with bombs and brains and courage!
—Softly, swiftly, at once be animal and angel—
But O no, no, they're Death's malkins dangling in the wire
  For the moon's interpretation.

PREPARATIONS FOR VICTORY

My soul, dread not the pestilence that hags
The valley; flinch not you, my body young,
At these great shouting smokes and snarling jags
Of fiery iron; as yet may not be flung
The dice that claims you. Manly move among
These ruins, and what you must do, do well;
Look, here are gardens, there mossed boughs are hung
With apples whose bright cheeks none might excel,
And there's a house as yet unshattered by a shell.

" I'll do my best," the soul makes sad reply,
" And I will mark the yet unmurdered tree,
The relics of dear homes that court the eye,
And yet I see them not as I would see.
Hovering between, a ghostly enemy
Sickens the light, and poisoned, withered, wan,
The least defiled turns desperate to me."
The body, poor unpitied Caliban,
Parches and sweats and grunts to win the name of Man.

Days or eternities like swelling waves
Surge on, and still we drudge in this dark maze,
The bombs and coils and cans by strings of slaves
Are borne to serve the coming day of days;
Pale sleep in slimy cellars scarce allays

With its brief blank the burden. Look, we lose;
The sky is gone, the lightless drenching haze
Of rainstorm chills the bone; earth, air are foes,
The black fiend leaps brick-red as life's last picture goes.

ZERO

O rosy red, O torrent splendour
   Staining all the Orient gloom,
O celestial work of wonder—
   A million mornings in one bloom!

What, does the artist of creation
   Try some new plethora of flame,
For his eye's fresh fascination?
   Has the old cosmic fire grown tame?

In what subnatural strange awakening
   Is this body, which seems mine?
These feet towards that blood-burst making,
   These ears which thunder, these hands which twine

On grotesque iron? Icy-clear
   The air of a mortal day shocks sense,
My shaking men pant after me here.
   The acid vapours hovering dense,

The fury whizzing in dozens down,
   The clattering rafters, clods calcined,
The blood in the flints and the trackway brown—
   I see I am clothed and in my right mind;

The dawn but hangs behind the goal.
   What is that artist's joy to me?
Here limps poor Jock with a gash in the poll,
   His red blood now is the red I see,

The swooning white of him, and that red!
    These bombs in boxes, the craunch of shells,
The second-hand flitting round; ahead!
    It's plain we were born for this, naught else.

AT SENLIS ONCE

O how comely it was and how reviving,
When with clay and with death no longer striving
    Down firm roads we came to houses
    With women chattering and green grass thriving.

Now though rains in a cataract descended,
We could glow, with our tribulation ended—
    Count not days, the present only
    Was thought of, how could it ever be expended?

Clad so cleanly, this remnant of poor wretches
Picked up life like the hens in orchard ditches,
    Gazed on the mill-sails, heard the church-bell,
    Found an honest glass all manner of riches.

How they crowded the barn with lusty laughter,
Hailed the pierrots and shook each shadowy rafter,
    Even could ridicule their own sufferings,
    Sang as though nothing but joy came after!

THE ZONNEBEKE ROAD

Morning, if this late withered light can claim
Some kindred with that merry flame
Which the young day was wont to fling through space!
Agony stares from each gray face.

And yet the day is come; stand down! stand down!
Your hands unclasp from rifles while you can,
The frost has pierced them to the bended bone?
Why, see old Stevens there, that iron man,
Melting the ice to shave his grotesque chin:
Go ask him, shall we win?
I never liked this bay, some foolish fear
Caught me the first time that I came in here;
That dugout fallen in awakes, perhaps,
Some formless haunting of some corpse's chaps.
True, and wherever we have held the line,
There were such corners, seeming-saturnine
   For no good cause.
                    Now where Haymarket starts,
That is no place for soldiers with weak hearts;
The minenwerfers have it to the inch.
Look, how the snowdust whisks along the road,
Piteous and silly; the stones themselves must flinch
In this east wind; the low sky like a load
Hangs over—a dead-weight. But what a pain
Must gnaw where its clay cheek
Crushes the shell-chopped trees that fang the plain—
The ice-bound throat gulps out a gargoyle shriek.
The wretched wire before the village line
Rattles like rusty brambles or dead bine,
And then the daylight oozes into dun;
Black pillars, those are trees where roadways run.
Even Ypres now would warm our souls; fond fool,
Our tour's but one night old, seven more to cool!
O screaming dumbness, O dull clashing death,
Shreds of dead grass and willows, homes and men,
Watch as you will, men clench their chattering teeth
And freeze you back with that one hope, disdain.

CONCERT PARTY: BUSSEBOOM

The stage was set, the house was packed,
  The famous troop began;
Our laughter thundered, act by act;
  Time light as sunbeams ran.

Dance sprang and spun and neared and fled,
  Jest chirped at gayest pitch,
Rhythm dazzled, action sped
  Most comically rich.

With generals and lame privates both
  Such charms worked wonders, till
The show was over—lagging loth
  We faced the sunset chill;

And standing on the sandy way,
  With the cracked church peering past,
We heard another matinée,
  We heard the maniac blast

Of barrage south by Saint Eloi,
  And the red lights flaming there
Called madness: Come, my bonny boy,
  And dance to the latest air.

To this new concert, white we stood;
  Cold certainty held our breath;
While men in the tunnels below Larch Wood
  Were kicking men to death.

RURAL ECONOMY (1917)

There was winter in those woods,
  And still it was July:
There were Thule solitudes
  With thousands huddling nigh;
There the fox had left his den,
The scraped holes hid not stoats but men.

To these woods the rumour teemed
  Of peace five miles away;
In sight, hills hovered, houses gleamed
  Where last perhaps we lay
Till the cockerels bawled bright morning and
The hours of life slipped the slack hand.

In sight, life's farms sent forth their gear;
  Here rakes and ploughs lay still;
Yet, save some curious clods, all here
  Was raked and ploughed with a will.
The sower was the ploughman too,
And iron seeds broadcast he threw.

What husbandry could outdo this?
  With flesh and blood he fed
The planted iron that nought amiss
  Grew thick and swift and red,
And in a night though ne'er so cold
Those acres bristled a hundredfold.

Why, even the wood as well as field
  This ruseful farmer knew
Could be reduced to plough and tilled,
  And if he planned, he'd do;
The field and wood, all bone-fed loam,
Shot up a roaring harvest-home.

E. W. T.: ON THE DEATH OF HIS
BETTY

And she is gone, whom, dream or truth,
You lived for in this wreck of youth,
    And on your brow sits age,
    Who's quickly won his siege.

My friend, you will not wish a word
Of striven help in this worst gird
    Of fortune as she gets
    From us our race's debts.

I see you with this subtlest blow
Like a stunned man softly go;
    Then you, love-baffled boy,
    Smile with a mournful joy.

Thereat I read, you plainly know
The time draws near when the fierce foe
    Shall your poor body tear
    And mix with mud and air.

Your smile is borne in that foredoom,
Beaten, you see your victory bloom,
    And fortune cheats her end,
    And death draws nigh, a friend.

BATTALION IN REST

Some found an owl's nest in the hollow skull
Of the first pollard from the malthouse wall;
    Some hurried through the swarming sedge
    About the ballast-pond's bright edge,

And flashed through sunny deeps like boys from school;
All was discovery, love and laughter all.

The girls along the dykes of those moist miles
Went on raft boats to take their cows afield,
   And eyes from many an English farm
   Saw and owned the mode had charm;
One well might mark the silence and the smiles;
With such sweet balms, our wounds must soon be healed.

The jovial sun sprang up as bright each day
As fancy's sun could be, and climbed, heaven's youth,
   To make the marching mornings cheat
   Still-hectoring Mars of his receipt—
Who cannot hear the songs that led the way,
See the trim companies with their eyes on truth?

At evening, by the lonely white-walled house,
Where Que-C'est-Drôle and Mon-Dieu stole to glance,
   One bold platoon all turned to players
   With masquerade and strumming airs;
The short clown darted nimble as a mouse,
The tambourine tapped out the stiff-stepped dance.

A shadowed corner suddenly found voice
As in the dusk I passed; it bade me stay.
   The bottle to my lips was raised—
   God help us, Serjeant, I was mazed
By that sharp fire your wine—but I rejoice!
Could I but meet you again at the end o' the day!

Not seldom, soft by meadows deep in dew,
Another lit my soul with his calm shine.
   There were cadences and whispers
   In his ways that made my vespers—
A night-piece fitting well that temple blue
Where stars new trembled with delight's design.

VLAMERTINGHE: PASSING THE CHATEAU, JULY 1917

"And all her silken flanks with garlands drest"—
But we are coming to the sacrifice.
Must those have flowers who are not yet gone West?
May those have flowers who live with death and lice?
This must be the floweriest place
That earth allows; the queenly face
Of the proud mansion borrows grace for grace
Spite of those brute guns lowing at the skies.

Bold great daisies, golden lights,
Bubbling roses' pinks and whites—
Such a gay carpet! poppies by the million;
Such damask! such vermilion!
But if you ask me, mate, the choice of colour
Is scarcely right; this red should have been much duller.

RECOGNITION

Old friend, I know you line by line,
    The touch, the tone, the turn of phrase,
Old autumn day, beloved and mine,
    Returning after many days;
The ten years' journey since we bade farewell
No hinted change or loss in you would ever tell.

Your countenance still ripe and kind
    Gazes upon me, godlike day,
And finding you again I find
    The tricks of time all thrown away.
The recollected turns to here and now
Beneath the equipoising glory of your brow.

P.M.Y.   145   K

Now to your heaven the gossamers gleam,
    Still soaring in their trembling play,
Their rosy scarves are spied astream;
    Whence borne and blown no one could say—
All out and dancing in the blue profound,
The tranquil ultimation of the ages round.

And here's that narrow orchard's grass,
    The last green luck for many a mile;
The patient lines of mules I pass,
    And then must stand and talk awhile
With gallant Maycock, spurred and gaitered, glowing
With this ripe sun, and red as any orchard growing.

This comrade, born to sow and stack,
    —A golden sheaf might seem his brother—
To-night will ride where the angry track
    Is death and ruin in a smother,
To-night I too must face the world's mad end—
But first we'll make this day, this godlike day our friend.

LA QUINQUE RUE

O road in dizzy moonlight bleak and blue,
With forlorn effigies of farms besprawled,
With trees bitterly bare or snapped in two,
Why riddle me thus—attracted and appalled?
For surely now the grounds both left and right
Are tilled, and scarless houses undismayed
Glow in the lustrous mercy of sweet night
And one may hear the flute or fiddle played.
Why lead me then
Through the foul-gorged, the cemeterial fen

146

To fear's sharp sentries? Why do dreadful rags
Fur these bulged banks, and feebly move to the wind?
That battered drum, say why it clacks and brags?
Another and another! what's behind?
How is it that these flints flame out fire's tongue,
Shrivelling my thought? these collapsed skeletons,
What are they, and these iron hunks among?
Why clink those spades, why glare these startling suns
And topple to the wet and crawling grass,
Where the strange briars in taloned hedges twine?
What need of that stopped tread, that countersign?
O road, I know those muttering groups you pass.
I know your way of turning blood to glass.
But, I am told, to-night you safely shine
    To trim roofs and cropped fields; the error's mine.

A. G. A. V.

Rest you well among your race, you who cannot be dead;
Sleep lives in that country place, sleep now, pillow your
    head;
Time has been you could not sleep, would not if you could,
But the relief stands in the keep where you so nobly stood.

Ardour, valour, the ceaseless plan all agreed to be yours,
Wit with these familiar ran, when you went to the wars;
If one cause I have for pride, it is to have been your friend,
To have lain in shell-holes by your side, with you to have
    seen impend

The meteors of the hour of fire, to have talked where speech
    was love,
Where through fanged woods and maw-gray mire the rain
    and murder drove;

There unchanged and on your mark you laughed at some
quaint clue,
And now, though time grows dull and dark, I hear, I bless
you anew.

Sleep—bless you, that would not please you, gallantest dear.
Should I find you beneath yew trees? better to look for
you here.
With those others whom well we knew, who went so
early away,
Will you not rather gladden my view? on a dead, deathless
day

Riding into the ancient town, smiling scarcely aware
Along the dale, over the down, into the drowsy square,
There to tarry in careless ways, in church, or shop, or inn,
Leisuring after fiery days; calm-shining, more than kin;

Though dim the guns of chaos roared upon the eastern
gate,
Though every hour the clock-hand scored brought closer a
desperate date—
Well shone you then, and I would will you freedom eternal
there,
Vast tumult past, and the proud sense still of vast to-
morrows to dare.

THEIR VERY MEMORY

Hear, O hear,
They were as the welling waters,
Sound, swift, clear,
They were all the running waters'
Music down the greenest valley.

148

Might words tell
What an echo sung within me?
What proud bell
Clangs a note of what within me
    Pealed to be with those enlisted?

When they smiled,
Earth's inferno changed and melted
    Greenwood mild;
Every village where they halted
    Shone with them through square and alley.

Now my mind
Faint and few records their showings,
    Brave, strong, kind—
I'd unlock you all their doings
    But the keys are lost and twisted.

This still grows,
Through my land or dull or dazzling
    Their spring flows;
But to think of them's a fountain,
    Tears of joy and music's rally.

ON READING THAT THE REBUILDING
OF YPRES APPROACHED COMPLETION

I hear you now, I hear you, shy perpetual companion,
Whose deep whispers
Never wholly failed upon my twilight; but for months
  now
Too dimly quivered
About the crowded corridors of purpose and the clamouring

Swarmed ingresses where like squinting cobblers and half-
  tailors
On a weary ship that moors in dock, with grimy hatches,
Cross-purpose jangles.

Those the master, with a sudden fountain anger, towering
By his mood a Cyclops,
Back has driven, back, and snivelling, cackling, down the
  ladder.
I, so springing,
Have lashed the buzzing bullies out, and in the freed air
  pause now,
Hearing you, whose face is ever one and ever million,
This dear dead one's, this dear living one's, no man's and
  all men's,
True map of Flanders.

Wordless language! well to me this moment making music,
Utmost union.
So, so, so we meet again; here we know our co-existence,
And your voice is
My self-utterance, while the region thus is hush and lonely,
Not a charlatan thought there left to gnaw my heart is
  skulking,
Nor one sunbeam sets the tingling atoms dancing by me
Like doubt's mad apings.

But my danger lies even here, even now worn weak and
  nerveless
I go drooping,
Heavy-headed, and would sleep thus lulled with your love's
  fulness.
Sharply awake me
With fierce words, cold as the fangs of bayonets in the
  frozen saps,
Simple as the fact that you must kill, or go for rations,

As clear as morning blue, as red and grotesque as the open
  mouths
Of winter corpses.

I hear you now: the voice, the voice of marching bowed
  battalions,
Of one strong soldier,
Now black-haired Daniells, now more saxon Clifford, now
  hale Worley—
O, speak. Our old tongue.
" I was Thy neighbour once, thou rugged Pile, thou white-
  ness, Ypres,
How mighty in thy misery, how royal in thy ravishing,
With fingers brittle as ice, I champed and clattered by the
  convent
And shouted orders;

Which echoes scrambling on the snowy walls and eyeless
  bulwarks
Made haste to carry,
But they could not, for the curious air was overburdened
With ancient echoes.
Vaults below the convent, when they pitied and would
  shelter,
Scarce could lure me, counter-lured though eyelids pressed
  like roof-leads;
Nor such sights as the circling pigeons of poor St. Martin
  held me
From my huge labours.

Blood-like swam the moon, the city's sable wounds lurked,
Still she cried out,
Be most constant! Thence with clumsy zeal and sacred cursing
Through the shrill grass,
Through the trapping thicket-thorns of death, that sudden
  planter,

While in the light of the moon and snow his blueness
    masked all faces,
Stern I went, the weaker kind most mercilessly heartening
To the shambles

All for her, that gap-toothed witch, that beauty at the
    butcher's,
To me intrusted;
Nor did I desert her, though without so much as a second's
    warning,
Some harsh slash-hook
Slit my skull and poured out all the fountains of my senses;
Burst the bloodgates; still I came, and went and came to
    man her,
Left Posthoornstraat and Goldfish Château, joined with
    waxen hands the cleft trench,
Hating and loving.

She, with that, was sometime mild and from the spectre ruin
Herself seemed lifting;
Walking in some silent moments, to the glimmer of candles,
I smiled and marvelled
How the dusky houses in the rainy gloom with feigned
    renaissance
Stood for life, and surely from the opened doors would be
    duly coming
Women and lightfoot children, lover there in the lamplight
    grow to lover—
Death, stop that laughing!

Nor has ever been the man, not Milton with his angels,
Who found such chorus,
Such diapason and amazement in strange old oriental
Fantasy-places,
As I in gross and clod-like names of hamlets by the city;

The fame of Kemmel clanged, and Athens dulled: I listened
If one spoke of Zonnebeke with thronged imagination,
A dazing distance.

For words spoke at the *Mermaid*, I would not give the
  meanest
That I heard echoing
In some green-shuttered *Nachtegaal* or *Kasteel*, a brief
  evening,
While the panes were jumping;
Far less one of the sweet astounding jests and sallies
That dared contest with smoking salvoes the forlorn hope's
  attention,
That wreathed the burning steel that slew with man's eternal
  laurel
In that one city.

For her was much accomplished, and she will not forget me,
Whose name is Legion;
She will know who knew her best, and with his rough
  warm garment
Would have wrapt her;
Her midnight tears will ever well as grayly she remembers
The hillock's signifying tree, that choked and gouged and
  miry
Was like a cross, but such a cross that there no bleeding
  Figure
Might hang without tautology.

And mine she is; they now may build, sign and assign there,
Above bright doorways
Paint in gold their titles; shrine among their tufted gardens,
As did their elders,
The statues of their mild desire Arcadian: but I
Am in the soil and sap, and in the becks and conduits

153

My blood is flowing, and my sigh of consummation
Is the wind in the rampart trees."

FLANDERS NOW

There, where before no master action struck
The grim Fate in the face, and cried " What now? ",
Where gain and commonplace lay in their ruck,
And pulled the beetroots, milked the muddy cow,
Heard the world's rumours, wished themselves good luck,
And slept, and rose, and lived and died somehow,—

A light is striking keen as angels' spears,
Brightness outwelling, cool as roses, there;
From every crossroad majesty appears,
Each cottage gleams like Athens on the air;
Ghosts by broad daylight, answered not by fears
But bliss unwordable, are walking there.

Who thirsts, or aches, or gropes as going blind?
Friend, drink with me at these fair-foliaged wells,
Or on the bruised life lay this unction kind,
Or mark this light that lives in lily-bells,
There rests and always shall the wandering mind,
Those clumsy farms to-day grow miracles:

Since past each wall and every common mark,
Field path and wooden bridge, there once went by
The flower of manhood, daring the huge dark,
The famished cold, the roaring in the sky;
They died in splendour, and they claimed no spark
Of glory save the light in a friend's eye.

THE WATCHERS

I heard the challenge " Who goes there? "
Close-kept but mine through midnight air;
I answered and was recognised
And passed, and kindly thus advised:
" There's someone crawlin' through the grass
By the red ruin, or there was,
And them machine guns been a firin'
All the time the chaps was wirin',
So sir if you're goin' out
You'll keep your 'ead well down no doubt."

When will the stern fine " Who goes there? "
Meet me again in midnight air?
And the gruff sentry's kindness, when
Will kindness have such power again?
It seems, as now I wake and brood,
And know my hour's decrepitude,
That on some dewy parapet
The sentry's spirit gazes yet,
Who will not speak with altered tone
When I at last am seen and known.

THE VISITOR

Suddenly the other side of this world wide,
Whose proud extent even conquering Steam allowed,
Grew near as the garden-gate; no mountain then,
No rosy-torturing desert, no dead lake,
Nor jungle, whirlpool, jealous frontier stopped us.
We moved within the wings of some ten words

Into a most familiar country air,
And like spring showers received it from the hills
That stood from our old hills ten thousand miles—
Or none; we paused along the yellow plains,
And kissed the child that ran from shyer friends
To take our hand; and we could tell what passed
In unknown language between old pouchy boat-men
Among the huge bulrushes where for ever
Dwells the uncaptured serpent six yards long,
Whom the small fish warping the waters' brim
Decline to notice. Then came orange-orchards,
Rising above the sea-cliff's bridle-roads;
And azure-flaming waves around rock-caves
Whence the pine thrust its elbows; then the dirge
Of sunless streams down cold black buttresses
Of vaster porticoes hurled up at heaven;
And then the patient mountain-stairs past peril,
Triumphant in the eyrie of a hamlet
That hears the constant silvering of the springs
And smiles in the mountain-steep among its cherries
Above the green air-crystal of the valley.

We knew them, we had seen the lights of evening
Moon-mimic here; and heard through dew-bells dim
The strings that men cicada-like set murmuring.
Here, cried our hearts, tune might be found at length,
And all our dust laved in this garden of waters,
Our hurry halted by these giant rocks,
Whose coldness is a kindness, and above
There should be purer beams from heaven;
                                    —no distance,
Sea, landslide, chasm, nor crossway of our life
Divided us that moment from the unknown
Pilgrimage singing in the stranger's mind.

THE QUICK AND THE DEAD

Once we three in Nara walked
Where pomp and fame look through the leaves;
With sabred shades we walked and talked
By lacquered gates and bow-like eaves,
By pools where carp doze through their green
Eternities, to lonelier shrines
Where mossy courtyards lie serene
Beneath some peasant-planted pines.

Less of that giant, surly bell
Whose black voice warned us at all hours
My late remembrance likes to tell,
Less of the Buddha as he lours
With thick curled skull and dead man's eye,
Of old wives' faithful groan of prayer,
Of fire-robed ritual trooping by,
Than the plain joy, three friends walked there.

THE INVIOLATE

There on the white Pacific shore the pines
  Still serve their jealous gods, and late and soon
The murmur runs along their rugged lines,
  " What black ship* waits the crash of our typhoon? "

And in this vigil circled, calm and proud,
  God-gates and temples glow with changeless noon,
Their mysteries awing that young seraph-cloud
  Swan-like between the mountain and the moon.

*Black ship, i.e. foreign warship as introduced by Commodore Perry.

THE AUTHOR'S LAST WORDS TO
HIS STUDENTS*

Forgive what I, adventuring highest themes,
　　Have spoiled and darkened, and the awkward hand
That longed to point the moral of man's dreams
　　And shut the wicket-gates of fairyland:
　　　　So by too harsh intrusion
　　　　Left colourless confusion.

For even the glories that I most revered,
　　Seen through a gloomed perspective in strange mood,
Were not what to our British seers appeared;
　　I spoke of peace, I made a solitude,
　　　　Herding with deathless graces
　　　　My hobbling commonplaces.

Forgive that eyeless lethargy which chilled
　　Your ardours and I fear dimmed much fine gold—
What your bright passion, leaping ages, thrilled
　　To find and claim, and I yet dared withhold;
　　　　These and all chance offences
　　　　Against your finer senses.

And I will ever pray for your souls' health,
　　Remembering how, deep-tasked yet eager-eyed,
You loved imagination's commonwealth,
　　Following with smiling wonder a frail guide
　　　　Who bears beyond the ocean
　　　　The voice of your devotion.

---

* In the school of English Literature, at the Tokyo Imperial University, 1924-1927.

FAMILIARITY

Dance not your spectral dance at me;
    I know you well!
Along this lane there lives no tree
    But I can tell.
I know each fall and rise and twist;
You—why, a wildflower in the mist,
    The moon, the mist.

Sound not that long alarm, gray tower,
    I know you well;
This is your habit at this hour,
    You and your bell!
If once, I heard a hundred times
Through evening's ambuscade your chimes—
    Dark tower, your chimes.

Enforce not that no-meaning so,
    Familiar stream;
Whether you tune it high or low,
    I know your theme;
A proud-fed but a puny rill,
A meadow brook, poured quick and shrill—
    Alone and shrill.

Sprawl not so monster-like, blind mist;
    I know not " seems ";
I am too old a realist
    To take sea-dreams
From you, or think a great white Whale
Floats through our hawthorn-scented vale—
    This foam-cold vale.

DREAM ENCOUNTERS

The measureless houses of dreams,
And the magic of hours within hours;
And those who pass by like clear streams,
Pass by us, on a journey not ours!
The eyes that we know and we fear,
As waters of Castaly clear,
That gaze that should once have been sweet,
Now a terror to meet!
—Yet both in one corridor narrowly led,
Those steps in another intensity tread;
There is space that convenes us, but holds us apart;
Sunlight and sunlight, distinctly combined,
As a wish with the wind
And all heaven with one heart.

PARABLE

Wide as the world is, music abounds;
Time has a legion of lovely sounds
From the soonest blackbird to latest bee
That murmurs along his honeying rounds;
  Surpassing those, one anthem is sweet
  As ever the message of Paraclete,
When the kiss of Spring
  Says all must sing
  And the host of secrets are bright on the wing.
Then the willow, that last in the moon stood numb,
Finds its Apollo-vesture come,
And, waiting on zephyr-sense so long,
Communes its sudden vein of song

Till on to the white and blue serene
One willow sings from a hamlet green.

Long are the sighs that lull the sleep
Of breathing youngness in such new hours.
Breezes are come to dance the flowers
But from what deep,
What siren shores!
Such nights, the moon's still self can stir
The feathery spray of this one tree,
And allure the least to tune with her—
She sways these leaves that sways the sea.
And far I hear the answer given;
Responding triumph will not pause,
Dares trespass the ethereal laws.
The ploughman's mark, the hatchet's toy,
Magicked into a wingèd Joy,
Reveals new song to Heaven.

A SUNRISE IN MARCH

While on my cheek the sour and savage wind
Confuses soul with sense, while unamazed
I view the siege of pale-starred horror raised
By dawn whose waves charge stern and crimson-lined,
In cold blue tufts of battle-smoke afar,
And sable crouching thickets by my way—
While I thus droop, the living land grows gay
With starry welcomes to the conquering star!

From every look-out whence they watch him win
(That angry Cromwell!) high on thorn and bine
The selfless wildbirds hail their holy light:

With changes free as flute or violin,
To naked fields they peal as proud and fine
As though they had not dreamed of death all night.

SUMMER RAINSTORM

Sweet conversations, woodland incantations
Are thrilling through the tides of gale and shower,
    Which now conceal,
    Now blue-reveal,
Across the fallow's russet undulations
A broken windmill and a silent tower.

And sometimes glancing through the top sprigs dancing
Elf-wings set out on visit and patrol.
    Though the full cloud
    Frowns monster-browed,
Those merry wild-folk chirruping and chancing
Know the kind truth; would I had such a soul!

Joy's masque and fashion of Time's Samson-passion
Deceives no lark that springs from weed and clod.
    Through their frank sight
    I feel the bright
Angel-event of sunset's fresh creation
And fields made lovely with the living God.

AUTUMN IN THE WEALD

Come, for here the lazy night
With rosy camp-fires blossoms bright,
The stream half-runs with flute-like trill
Through the quaint channels of the mill

And, to accentuate the hush,
Through fine bamboo and needled rush
A water-spirit ferries. Come,
And see how kindly all's at home.
No sweeter things than these I rhyme,
And this by much their sweetest time.
Then, sweet, agree, and by this gate
Watch each one gathering to his mate,
To nest or warren, bough or byre—
The dearness answers all desire,
When all, the shepherd, dog and sheep
With sleep-like motions welcome sleep;
The elm-tree's momentary stir
And freshened sluices yield to her,
And though the fire-side shout and song
Defy her there, they will not long.

The bonfire's crackling zeal dies down,
   The laughing supper-groups are gone,
The fair falls quiet in Yalding town,
   Alone with the mist I linger on.

RETURN

Deed and event of prouder stature
   Dare not always overshade
The first fresh buddings of our nature;
   Their hidden colour does not fade.

We well may quit our laboured action
   At some sweet call to early loves,
And find the jewel of self-contraction
   Like saints in rocks and springs and groves.

163

Win back the world when true Aurora
    Dawned a goddess, not an hour!
Think, have you caught the smile of Flora
    Since your own life was a young flower?

And Love, even Love, has dropped her lilies
    On the hot highroad; once she knew
How columbines and daffadillies
    Created her own sun and dew.

Return; how stands that man enchanted
    Who, after seas and mountains crossed,
Finds his old threshold, so long scanted,
    With not a rose or robin lost!

The wise, from passion now retreating
    To the hamlets of the mind,
In every glance have claimed the greeting
    Of spirits infinitely kind.

THE DEEPER FRIENDSHIP

Were all eyes changed, were even poetry cold,
Were those long systems of hope that I tried to deploy
Skeletons, still I should keep one final hold,
Since clearer and clearer returns my first-found joy.

I would go, once more, through the sunless autumn in
    trouble;
Thin and cold rain dripping down through branches black,
Streams hoarse-hurrying and pools spreading over the
    stubble,
And the waggoner leaving the hovel under his sack

Would guide me along by the gate and deserted siding,
The inn with the tattered arbour, the choking weir;
And yet, security there would need small guiding.
I know one hearth, one love that shine beyond fear.

There, though the sharpest storm and flood were abroad,
And the last husk and leaf were stripped from the tree,
I would sue for peace where the rats and mice have gnawed,
And well content that Nature should bury me.

THE BLIND LEAD THE BLIND

Dim stars like snowflakes are fluttering in heaven,
Down the cloud-mountains by wind-torrents riven;
There are still chances, but one more than all
Slowly burns out on the sea's dark wall—
    The best ever given.

One, the divinest, goes down to the dark,
In a red sullen vanishing, a poor stifled spark.
You, who have reason, were staring at this
As though by your gaze it would clear the abyss—
    It was once your sea-mark.

Hear on the shore too the sighed monotones
Of waves that in weakness slip past the purled stones;
The seethe of blown sand round the dry fractured hull,
Salt-reeds and tusked fence; hear the struck gull
    With death in his bones.

Slow comes the net in, that's filled with frustration;
Night ends the day of thwart discreation;
I would be your miracle-worker, sad friend,
Bid a music for you and a new star ascend,—
    But I know isolation.

REPORT ON EXPERIENCE

I have been young, and now am not too old;
And I have seen the righteous forsaken,
His health, his honour and his quality taken.
　This is not what we were formerly told.

I have seen a green country, useful to the race,
Knocked silly with guns and mines, its villages vanished,
Even the last rat and last kestrel banished—
　God bless us all, this was peculiar grace.

I knew Seraphina; Nature gave her hue,
Glance, sympathy, note, like one from Eden.
I saw her smile warp, heard her lyric deaden;
　She turned to harlotry;—this I took to be new.

Say what you will, our God sees how they run.
These disillusions are His curious proving
That He loves humanity and will go on loving;
　Over there are faith, life, virtue in the sun.

EPITAPH

Happily through my years this small stream ran;
It charmed the boy, and purified the man;
Its hollowed banks were my romantic caves,
Its winter tumults made my ocean waves.
I had no gold, nor silver overmuch,
But what its sunny falls disclosed as such,
And wished no gem, when eyes could here be bright
With the kingfisher's sapphire beam of flight,

Or the pearl shield that tilting fish below
Through arras of blue water-mosses show.
What need for templed lotus, when our stream
Enthroned the yellow lily? here the dream
Of placid Buddha might be as secure;
Visitant wings there were that loved the lure.

With all my years this pretty stream sang on.
I brought one here to praise it; who is gone,
Yet in that crystal soul her mirrored face
With foxgloves looking in still finds a place.
Even the Muse's " melody unheard "
For me is woven with this water's word,
Since here I sat to read immortal song;
The ripple played to that, nor answered wrong.
All that deep-sighing elegy might mourn,
Glad lyric hail, and sonnet-thought adorn,
The changeful rivulet from stone to stone
Enchanted into anthems of its own.

My travel then! my wealth, my dream, my love
True Golden Treasury and Golden Grove!
Accept one weakness, let one pale shade cling
Where with so strong a life you run and sing.

A CONNOISSEUR

Presume not that gray idol with the scythe
And hourglass of the stern perpetual sands
To be a mere insensate mill of hours,
Unawed by battles, unbeguiled with flowers;
Think, this old Merlin may be vexed or blithe,
And for the future stretches hungry hands.

167

No last year's bride discovers more caprice
Than this bald magpie smuggling up his wit,
And in his crumbling belfry, where the cost
Of high-born death in plundered ruin's lost,
Nodding his glory to each glittering piece
Of glass or jewel that his fancy hit.

Close in the shop of some lean artizan,
Who carves a snuff-box for Squire Harkaway,
Time stoops, and stares, and knows his destined prize:
Crœsus shall hunt this modest merchandise
When frieze and pillar of a master's plan
Are crushed in waggon-tracks to bind the clay.

There stalled theology makes angels weep
In twenty volumes blazoned red and gold,
And there a broadside's bawled about the street;
Time fetched his halfpence out and bought a sheet.
The twenty volumes slumber in a heap,
The ballad among heirlooms lives enrolled.

Lordly oration thronged the sculptured roof,
And pamphleteered in plaudits through the town;
The charlatan proclaimed his draughts and pills,
And tossed the crowd his woodcuts and his bills;
From rhetoric's remains Time flies aloof,
And hears the quack still pattering to the clown.

Voluptuous canvas! Venus in May-bloom,
Sunshine of vital gold, faun-twinkling groves,
Harmonious limbs and volant veils, go mourn;
For you will lie with fire, while Time has borne
The blue-daubed frigate from the servants' room
To swell the mad collection of his loves.

THE STUDY

While I sit penning plans of dead affairs,
And hardly pause but when some wilder gust
Drives the mist shower with a more savage thrust
Against my window, hark! what sweeter cares
Find a shy voice, that makes my writing cease,
And in this room of shelves, and books, and files,
The ranked and crested past, what pleasure smiles!
The dead withdraw, the living shares their peace,

For down my chimney with the dripping rain
Come tiny trills and chirps and silvery notes
Like whistling mice; it's nesting-time again;
There in the dimness gape what eager throats
Of the new brood, who through this tempest dun
Know they are for the singing and the sun!

VALUES

Till darkness lays a hand on these gray eyes
And out of man my ghost is sent alone,
It is my chance to know that force and size
Are nothing but by answered undertone.
No beauty even of absolute perfection
Dominates here—the glance, the pause, the guess
Must be my amulets of resurrection;
Raindrops may murder, lightnings may caress.

There I was tortured, but I cannot grieve;
There crowned and palaced—visibles deceive.
That storm of belfried cities in my mind
Leaves me my vespers cool and eglantined.

From love's wide-flowering mountain-side I chose
This sprig of green, in which an angel shows.

AN ANCIENT GODDESS

IN TWO PICTURES

I

The time grows perilous; forth she comes once more,
The ghost, the dying lady and dead star;
Empress and votaress, to whom the roar
Of ocean towers from many a reef and bar,
Nor less love's whispering dares respond so far;
She comes, upon whose tombless face have I
Gazed long in statued muteness singular,
These eyes enchanted by that inward eye;
What tragic Need impels this ghost into our sky?

Herself impels and moves the life we know,
But whither? in what thought? To what sad grove
Guides she the stolen spirit? When the glow
Of morning clothes us, up spring joy and love;
The sunbeam is perennial treasure-trove.
The sun's a triumph, and his laughing zest
Round the world's homesteads huntsman-like arove
Makes man much more the man. This other quest
Lures out the voiceless bird, unwarms the empty nest.

Veiled now in violet wreathes she gliding mocks
The taken sense; what frown, what mal-ease there!
She is but dusty seas and steely rocks,
She is a brooding badness in the air.

But while we speak, we think afresh, nor dare
   Assail what so intrinse and magic dwells
In the night's breast. And soon all snow-white there
   Palely she moves. That paleness nothing tells.
Unknowable, she passes all our sentinels.

II

Above the whole world, walking the blue space
Where many worlds are pale or glittering wheeled,
We know that Phœbe dotes upon this place,
This tiny place, this lodging in the field,
   Dearest of all; so calmly yearning
     She holds the open sky,
   And every crevice, path and turning
     Lures her love-diffusing eye
Till all with not a little joy confess
They are the chosen of that loveliness.

There is a sluice through whose rude-masoned stones
And fissured planks our timid river falls.
Day with his loud light quells his watery tones,
But hear him now! as though a sea-god calls:
   Hushed then awhile, then tide-like booming—
     The hill-top wanderer hears,
   And she on high, without fault blooming,
     In his shadowed crystal peers,
And fishes rise that in the silver blaze
Hurl their new sheen and diamonded rays.

Meanwhile the woods with ichor in their limbs
Wake in a dance of slow religious love;
A whispering music in this spinney brims,
Floats heavenward; fades; then answers that great grove.

Youth here with light and eager greeting
    And age with museful sighs
In tune and order claim the meeting
    With the enchantress of the skies—
All, all our valley, to the tiniest flowers,
And shyest wings, is singing, She is ours.

Nor could she touch with fonder glad caress
Even the churl outlands of our country homes.
Conceive you cannot that such pleasantness
Smiles on unmerit when from here she roams:
    The ridge so flinty and so boorish
        Seems a bosom dreaming warm,
    The swamp sharp-sworded, bleak and moorish,
        Glows like lamplight from a farm,
And even the condemned house reveals a bloom
Hovering like pity in each suspect room.

In our kind cottages the babies wake,
At once with hasty fear the mothers raise
Their patient heads; then not a sound they make,
For beautiful's the infant in amaze
    At latticed moonlight, branching holy
        Upon the fairy wall;
    The child voice musically and lowly
        With a new note, a bird call,
Increases what appeared past all increase,
And deepens even the mother's love and peace.

More wonders yet in this our lucky vale,
When the moon marks and clasps it for her joy!
Have we not seen, when moon and nightingale
Enlustred the green season, some young boy

Beside the old tower's solemn stature
   At watch, in heaven alone,
As though this night ancestral nature
   Called him there to make it known
That he in after-time should find such hours
A moonlit sanctuary from time's worst powers?

WINTER NIGHTS

A BACKWARD LOOK

Strange chord! the weir-pool's tussling dance.
   Curt crows, and a pleading bell;
While westward day with a mænad glance
   Bids the blue-lipped floods farewell.
The star-led enemy airs begin
   To prowl in a deadly crawl,
And along these village parapets thin
   Swoops Night like the end of all.

Black amphitheatre, eyeless Shades
   That stalk the monstrous stage,
Here vainly descend your ghostly raids
   And measureless icy rage!
Here village blood to the threat in the air
   Responds with sparkling streams,
And here and there and everywhere
   Humanity's victory beams.

See Peter in the latticed loft
   Put the last of his work away;
His mood—the apple-scent not so soft,
   And the lantern's honey ray
173

So paints his cheek, that the urchin lad
  That haunts him whenever he can
Copies his tread, and calls him dad,
  And feels ten times a man.

In the inn the creased young shopman shines
  At the lancers and quadrilles,
Up and down, in and out the smiling lines
  His twinkling courtesy thrills
Lavinia here, Amelia there—
  Their blushes flower in pleasure,
And smoothing back their straying hair
  They enchant themselves with the measure.

Or perhaps on the candled platform stands
  The carpenter of the place,
Gripping his songbook with both hands;
  To the piano's strumming bass
He venturing adds his woodnotes wild;
  We applaud the patriot feeling,
And, flats and sharps so reconciled,
  We " list the music stealing."

Often again in the flame-like cold
  The church's rustling aisles
Are beset with quiring young and old
  For whom Christ's coming smiles:
" On Jordan's banks "—O how the rose
  Breaks red from each dusty tomb,
And the team from the *Bull* come proudly to pull
  Their bells as Christ nears home.

Midwinter mirth! the magic of earth;
  The threadbare soul rejoices
And glittering hears by time's hoarse weirs
  Through the rain those honest voices;
The red-screened windows of schoolhouse and inn

Dart life through the moorlands raw,
And the lovetalk, carolling, dancing din,
Are the heart's invincible law.

KINGFISHER

The eastern God with natural blessing gleams
Upon our temple of another faith,
And wakes our world; our hills, our streams,
Farms, anvils all begin afresh. Each wraith
That even in this sweet glade
Clings with the bat and moth below night's covert shade
Is sent away; fast flit the shoal
Of water-ghosts, they end their white patrol
Of foam-flowered whirlpools; none deny
That ancient, sharp, and fearless Eye.
Yet here, as morning takes in her young hands
The lilies, and to gild her coloured bands
Desires those sunny flashes from the swim
Of naiad-ripples over the warm sands,
Or where the wave looks cherry-ripe or blue
In its fair answer to the flowery shore,
An eye peers through
The willow-lattice, capturing much more
My fancy; while on that green farther ledge
The gray mare bites the alder and cool sedge,
This eye across the wide clear river burns,
And in the rosy glass of bloom discerns.
Then sapphire lightning falls, the waters burst,
The lightning leaps reversed,
And with his eye's quick distant prize
The kingfisher returns.

PREMATURE REJOICING

What's that over there?
Thiepval Wood.
Take a steady look at it; it'll do you good.
Here, these glasses will help you. See any flowers?
There sleeps Titania (correct—the Wood is ours);
There sleeps Titania in a deep dugout,
Waking, she wonders what all the din's about,
And smiles through her tears, and looks ahead ten years,
And sees her Wood again, and her usual Grenadiers,
    All in green,
    Music in the moon;
The burnt rubbish you've just seen
Won't beat the Fairy Queen;
    All the same, it's a shade too soon
    For you to scribble rhymes
    In your army book
    About those times;
    Take another look;
That's where the difficulty is, over there.

CHANCES OF REMEMBRANCE

I

"Turn not from me;
I am the last rainbow that you may ever see.
    Take the rich surprise
    Of the skies
    With all your eyes;
Dream from what labyrinths of bloom my wings arise.—
    See,
    Even a rainbow dies."

" You see me here,
  And you huddle past and shiver;
    One glance, you disappear,
Leaving me, a dull brown thicket, beside a gray-gorged river.
    I beg no grace of yours;
You have seen me, I go with you, in or out of doors;
    My thin blood will not wash out,
    My purple brambles will mantle you about,
    My thorny claspings pierce
    Into your verse."

THE SUNLIT VALE

I saw the sunlit vale, and the pastoral fairy-tale;
The sweet and bitter scent of the may drifted by;
And never have I seen such a bright bewildering green,
    But it looked like a lie,
    Like a kindly meant lie.

When gods are in dispute, one a Sidney, one a brute,
It would seem that human sense might not know, might
    not spy;
But though nature smile and feign where foul play has
    stabbed and slain,
    There's a witness, an eye,
    Nor will charms blind that eye.

Nymph of the upland song and the sparkling leafage young,
For your merciful desire with these charms to beguile,
For ever be adored; muses yield you rich reward;
    But you fail, though you smile—
    That other does not smile.

The impulses of April, the rain-gems, the rose-cloud,
The frilling of flowers in the westering love-wind!
And here through the Park come gentlemen riding,
And there through the Park come gentlemen riding,
And behind the glossy horses Newfoundland dogs follow.
Says one dog to the other, " This park, sir, is mine, sir."
The reply is not wanting; hoarse clashing and mouthing
Arouses the masters.
Then Colonel Montgomery, of the Life Guards, dismounts.
" Whose dog is this?" The reply is not wanting,
From Captain Macnamara, Royal Navy: " My dog."
" Then call your dog off, or by God he'll go sprawling."
" If my dog goes sprawling, you must knock me down
      after."
" Your name?" " Macnamara, and yours is——" " Mont-
      gomery."
" And why, sir, not call your dog off?" " Sir, I chose
Not to do so, no man has dictated to me yet,
And you, I propose, will not change that." " This place,
For adjusting disputes, is not proper"—and the Colonel,
Back to the saddle, continues, " If your dog
Fights my dog, I warn you, I knock your dog down.
For the rest, you are welcome to know where to find me,
Colonel Montgomery; and you will of course
Respond with the due information." " Be sure of it."

Now comes the evening, green-twinkling, clear-echoing,
And out to Chalk-farm the Colonel, the Captain,
Each with his group of believers, have driven.
      Primrose Hill on an April evening
          Even now in a fevered London
      Sings a vesper sweet; but these
      Will try another music. Hark!

These are the pistols; let us test them; quite perfect.
Montgomery, Macnamara six paces, two faces;
Montgomery, Macnamara—both speaking together
In nitre and lead, the style is incisive,
Montgomery fallen, Macnamara half-falling,
The surgeon exploring the work of the evening—
And the Newfoundland dogs stretched at home in the fire-
	light.

The coroner's inquest; the view of one body;
And then, pale, supported, appears at Old Bailey
James Macnamara, to whom this arraignment:
	You stand charged
	That you
	With force and arms
	Did assault Robert Montgomery,
	With a certain pistol
	Of the value of ten shillings,
	Loaded with powder and a leaden bullet,
	Which the gunpowder, feloniously exploded,
	Drove into the body of Robert Montgomery,
	And gave
	One mortal wound;
	Thus you did kill and slay
	The said Robert Montgomery.

O heavy imputation! O dead that yet speaks!
O evening transparency, burst to red thunder!

Speak, Macnamara. He, tremulous as a windflower,
Exactly imparts what had slaughtered the Colonel.
" Insignificant the origin of the fact now before you;
Defending our dogs, we grew warm; that was nature;
That heat of itself had not led to disaster.
From defence to defiance was the leap that destroyed.

At once he would have at my deity, Honour—
' If you are offended you know where to find me.'
On one side, I saw the wide mouths of Contempt,
Mouth to mouth working, a thousand vile gunmouths;
On the other my Honour; Gentlemen of the Jury,
I am a Captain in the British Navy."

Then said Lord Hood: " For Captain Macnamara,
He is a gentleman and so says the Navy."
Then said Lord Nelson: " I have known Macnamara
Nine years, a gentleman, beloved in the Navy,
Not to be affronted by any man, true,
Yet as I stand here before God and my country,
Macnamara has never offended, and would not,
Man, woman, child." Then a spring-tide of admirals,
Almost Neptune in person, proclaim Macnamara
Mild, amiable, cautious, as any in the Navy;
And Mr. Garrow rises, to state that if need be,
To assert the even temper and peace of his client,
He would call half the Captains in the British Navy.

Now we are shut from the duel that Honour
Must fight with the Law; no eye can perceive
The fields wherein hundreds of shadowy combats
Must decide between a ghost and a living idolon—
A ghost with his army of the terrors of bloodshed,
A half-ghost with the grand fleet of names that like sunrise
Have dazzled the race with their march on the ocean.

Twenty minutes. How say you?
                              Not guilty.

Then from his chair with his surgeon the Captain
Walks home to his dog, his friends' acclamations
Supplying some colour to the pale looks he had,
Less pale than Montgomery's; and Honour rides on.

THE KISS

I am for the woods against the world,
    But are the woods for me?
I have sought them sadly anew, fearing
    My fate's mutability.
Or that which action and process make
    Of former sympathy.

Strange that those should arrive strangers
    Who were once entirely at home.
Colonnade, sunny wall and warren,
    Islet, osier, foam,
Buds and leaves and selves seemed
    Safe to the day of doom.

By-roads following, and this way wondering,
    I spy men abroad
In orchards, knarred and woody men
    Whose touch is bough and bud;
Co-arboreal sons of landscape.
    Then in the windstript wood

Is the cracking of stems; and under the thorn
    With a kobold's closeness lurks
The wanderer with his knife and rods,
    That like a bald rook works;
His woman-rook about the thicket
    Prowls at the hazel-forks.

Sheep lying out by the swollen river
    Let the flood roll down
Without so much as a glance; they know it;
    The hurling seas of brown
Cannot persuade the ferrying moorhen
    Her one willow will drown.

This way wondering, I renew
        Some sense of common right;
And through my armour of imposition
        Win the Spring's keen light,
Till for the woods against the world
        I kiss the aconite.

FANCY AND MEMORY

Adieu, young Fancy with the gipsy eye,
Sly slip of a ghost, your time with me is done;
Once we were bold together, now good-bye,
Once you lit heaven, I now prefer the sun:
Flit on, delicious false one, and still please
The hearts you may awhile; bring Sullen to his knees.

Your sister Memory is more welcome now.
She if she feigns at all seems without guile;
She tells no tale for time to disavow,
No contraries but she will reconcile;
With her I wonder less than love, and calm
Comes with no greater stir than dewy nightflowers' balm.

She makes the tiny nautilus sail sweet
Upon the shell-smooth lulling ocean-stream;
And men who died arise and smile to see't,
And I am free to talk of life with them;
She gives me temple-steps in warm west rain,
The crystal summit, thunderous pinewood, ripening plain.

Music she has that richly speaks her mind;
So singing, she with Orpheus vies; I hear,
And Flemish church-tower vanes glint in the wind
And man and horse and crow again live near,—
Man, horse, and guns and mines and tanks renew
Daybreak's demented duel—Memory, *et tu*?

THE MEMORIAL, 1914-1918

Against this lantern, shrill, alone
The wind springs out of the plain.
Such winds as this must fly and moan
Round the summit of every stone
On every hill; and yet a strain
Beyond the measure elsewhere known
Seems here.
    Who cries? who mingles with the gale?
Whose touch, so anxious and so weak, invents
A coldness in the coldness? in this veil
Of whirling mist what hue of clay consents?
Can atoms intercede?

And are those shafted bold constructions there,
Mines more than golden, wheels that outrace need,
Crowded corons, victorious chimneys—are
Those touched with question too? pale with the dream
Of those who in this aether-stream
Are urging yet their painful, woundful theme?

Day flutters as a curtain, stirred
By a hidden hand; the eye grows blurred.
Those towers, uncrystalled, fade.
The wind from north and east and south
Comes with its starved white mouth
And at this crowning trophy cannot rest—
No, speaks as something past plain words distressed.

Be still, if these your voices are; this monolith
For you and your high sleep was made.
Some have had less.
No gratitude in deathlessness?
No comprehension of the tribute paid?

You would speak still? Who with?

We talked of ghosts; and I was still alive;
And I that very day was thirty-five;
Alone once more, I stared about my room
And wished some ghost would be a friend and come;
I cared not of what shape or semblance; terror
Was nothing in comparison with error;
I wished some ghost would come, to talk of fate,
And tell me why I drove my pen so late,
And help with observations on my knack
Of being always on the bivouac,
Here and elsewhere, for ever changing ground,
Finding and straightway losing what I found,
Baffled in time, fumbling each sequent date,
Mistaking Magdalen for the Menin Gate.
This much I saw without transmortal talk,
That war had quite changed my sublunar walk—
Forgive me, dear, honoured and saintly friends;
Ingratitude suspect not; this transcends.
Forgive, O sweet red-smiling love, forgive,
If this is life, for your delight I live;
How every lamp, how every pavement flames
Your beauty at me, and your faith acclaims!
But from my silences your kindness grew,
And I surrendered for the time to you,
And still I hold you glorious and my own,
I'd take your hands, your lips; but I'm alone.
So I was forced elsewhere, and would accost
For colloquy and guidance some kind ghost.
As one that with a serious trust was sent
Afar, and bandits seized him while he went,
And long delayed, so I; I yearned to catch
What I should know before my grave dispatch

Was to be laid before that General
Who in a new Time cries " backs to the wall."
No ghost was granted me; and I must face
Uncoached the masters of that Time and Space,
And there with downcast murmurings set out
What my gross late appearance was about.

ANOTHER ALTAR

I am Forgetfulness. I am that shadow
Of whom well warned you thought your pathway clear,
You need sharp eyes to catch such silent shadows.
Not all your wakeful plans and resolution
Outsoldiered me; you heard me at last low-laughing,
" When the steed's stolen, shut the stable-door."
This, too, is nothing of mine. No sly ambition
Nor malice moves me; but my part is fixed
In changing onward life from scene to scene,
Necessitating futures of surprise,
Solving some enigmas, much preserving
To bloom a wonder in a way the sowers
Could never have guessed. I touch the cells of the mind,
And some are by that finger barred and bolted;
It may be but a moment that I triumph;
Consider what my moments still achieve.

Through me the wife learns who the mistress is,
And where. I trap the assassin, and safe murder
Becomes a dance on air. One look from me
And the mind's eye of the signalman is dimmed
And wreckage piles and flames above the dead.
I have contrived that some most secret treasures
Shall lie an age untouched, and late-discovered

Should be the source of hope and peace; I leave
The child's toy to become posterity's marvel,
From lost Tanagra; this quaint poniard lurked
Under my influence, where the culprit stowed it,
To tell man something of his martyrdoms,
Upon a day. From these my hoarded papers
At length uncovered, an impoverished fame
Grows full and noonday-clear; with that, your scholar
Is charmed with joys not his, and shall not fail
Of praise and proud remembrance—while I will.
Be sure, unsure of most, that I will make
An instrument of you this very day,
That I may weave my share of Then and Now,
A web that greater gods design—with me.
He that now writes the words I whisper to him
Has here and there unknowingly surrendered
To my caprice, if so he please to style it,
And will still find his early morning again,
Through me, after a dry and droughty journey,
All fresh and violet-dewy; he, at least,
Will not disdain to bow to me as one
Among the more ingenious undergods.

A CALM RAIN

" Come, shy and almost-silent rain;
Low-whisperer, all thy reminiscence yield
   Across this field,
Among these houses come, and kiss this flower;
Befall me with the secret of Verlaine
That answered thee so well, and answering thee was healed;
Or thy dim veil will bring me a long hour
Of twilight listening under Eastern eaves
For breathing leaves

That loved thy coming too, and the crossroad stone
Once made a god, that stood afield alone
And to thy touch seemed as a brow renewed
By infancy's or love's beatitude.
Moving as now thou dost, thy tender power
Defeating time's hard march has called the halt,
And in this nook made union without fault
Of places, senses, wonderings, O pale shower,
That seemed asunder; mountains and sands and seas,
And cliffs and chasms of life, had parted these;
My soul lost hold of what had been, beyond,
As though there were none but a racial bond
Between her and the former friend to thee,
That even in war's corruptions sang to thee,
And found thee true in fiery pits that leapt
In blood and wounds, and knew one angel wept,
Last naked hearths and newest graves were thine,
I wooed thy word, I had thy sign."

So this still rain beguiled my mood and verse,
But I awake; I dreamed; what worth is his
Who fashions thus a selfish universe,
And weaves dead leaves with living tragedies?
While the strong world goes forth in symphonies
Of action, passion, science and resource,
Where shall faint music and far similes
Befriend it? has this stealing shower a force?
And yet I fancy sometimes there is pain
That still requires this shy and dream-like rain.

DESIRE AND DELIGHT

Desire, the lovelier prophet of delight!
    Forerunner from whose starry look
    The world a rarer meaning took
Than ever lived in the consequence, though bright:

Dreamer of marvellous venture, music, creed,
    Still triumph; not to thee the blame
    If thine announcèd lack thy flame,
And after thee prove but a broken reed.

A NIGHT-PIECE

From the Greek of Alcman

Asleep; the pinnacles and the precipices of the mountains,
Headlands, and torrents, and all that walk and creep
On the shadowy earth that breeds them; the beasts that
    haunt in the mountains,
The world of bees, the kraken in the blue deep;
Even the orders of birds of widest wing are asleep.

THE TOWER

Stone ghost,
Dispel your mantled muteness, though no breath
Ripples your elms to a sigh.
Speak on the air auspicious now, my wraith,
End midday's pause with a cry

Whence all your centuries shall seize my soul.
Sing me the loveliest, wildest, furthermost;
And, as your voice were lightning-flash, outroll
Time's darkened country in intense reliefs,
Your flinty joys and griefs,—
Since black-stoled saints, watched by the wood's sharp eyes,
First set your foot firm in the fosse,
And droning slow gaunt hymns, uplifted you strong into
    space.

The day came when the builders were not, when the
    trampled chace
Pealed no quick chisel-blow; then the sly moss
Stole on the roods where no church now would ever arise.

Resound the dins of skirmishes
And dangerous verdure; when green shade
Might bark with gun, or gleam with blade,
And hooves through bells of lilies pashed,
And helmets and cuirasses flashed
From ambuscade to man to man,
And who stood fast, and who ran,
Which shook the sparrows from seed and grain,
And struck blue sparks along the lane.

I hear that stroke which tore
Your tamped bell-stair with a rocking roar,
And see, from tales of neighbouring folk,
Figures with hands that claw the smoke;
But there's a theme, old tower, that we'll alone explore.

Rather in this be heard, even now fulfil
Your better tune, that grew from years and years
Of Autumn's binding sheaves on the round hill,
And rich drowsed hours between, some gossamers

Restless alone in that blue peace; or, if you will,
Renew the sense how spring at first
Dances along each stream that talks and trolls
Among a paradise of flowers; or June athirst
Slips to the wood dyke where the hedgehog lolls
A harmless goblin twined about with wreaths of white
  bell-bind.

Yet, if your stern stone mind
Like none of these, nor peace nor pastoral mood,
Then cry some storm's prodigious brood,
In vast and shattered wood,
That had all through your recollection stood;
Or thunder's wrath, whose finger strikes
The royal oaks to cindered spikes;
Cry wings of winter-winds that surge
From the inhuman Northern verge
Of life, cry as the iron sky
Will sometimes cry.

For here to you,
Stone ghost that hear so much from stars and storms,
Whose brow the first beam of the morning warms
And whose deformity to kingship grew,
Some have been in enchantment and in consolation led,—
To you who never with remindful scorn
Tolled out the lives of all that breathe to mourn,
And shade no darling dead.

LONG MOMENTS

A shadow lay along my wall
    Like a shark in a sandy bay,
And on my mind a yellow dullness
    Lay, and lay, and lay,
Yet from the wall I could not will
    My eyes away.

Messages came from the simple world
    Of the village beyond the wall,
The clink of work and bell of time
    And stroke of bat and ball,
But nothing stirred the weed which wove
    My mind and the shadow on the wall,

Until from years and years before
    From a day that had looked dead gray,
Another dullness and stagnant silence,
    Came an inward ray
That over ghostly roofs now drew
    My soul away.

THE SURPRISE

Shot from the zenith of desire
    Some faultless beams found where I lay,
Not much expecting such white fire
    Across a slow close working-day.

What a great song then sang the brook,
    The fallen pillar's grace how new;
The vast white oaks like cowslips shook—
    And I was winged, and flew to you.

191

THE COTTAGE AT CHIGASAKI

That well you draw from is the coldest drink
In all the country Fuji looks upon;
And me, I never come to it but I think
The poet lived here once who one hot noon
Came dry and eager, and with wonder saw
The morning-glory* about the bucket twined,
Then with a holy heart went out to draw
His gallon where he might; the poem's signed
By him and Nature. We need not retire,
But freely dip, and wash away the salt
And sand we've carried from the sea's blue fire;
Discuss a melon; and without great fault,
Though comfort is not poetry's best friend,
We'll write a poem too, and sleep at the end.

REFLECTIONS

Mirror of wall and tree, of cloud and star,
Still making phantoms, wooing us passing by
To droop our look from the summer sky
And the ornament of the sparkling air,
Enchanted with thy copy! The lovely lie
Has a strange calm in't. Those trees have no zeal
Of tragic glory, breathe no life, no death
In their cool dusky sprays—the scattered curls
Of roses float there, but no contact find.
These, having neither blood nor breath,
No voice to raise, no wound to heal,
Are kinder than the kind.

* Perhaps the most familiar Japanese poem is that which says, approximately,
" The morning-glory has taken hold of the well-bucket; I'll borrow some water
elsewhere."

LARK DESCENDING

A singing firework; the sun's darling;
    Hark how creation pleads!
Then silence: see, a small gray bird
    That runs among the weeds.

A THOUGHT OF THE DOWNS

Come now, my love without whom nothing wakes,
    My Sylva, let me show
    Something of what I owe
To your discovering dearness; my mind breaks
The barriers of the hour and task,—we stand
Delighted, arm in arm, to spy the land
That in its amphitheatre includes
    Fallows, and cores, and brown-tiled spires, and dells,
Elm-colonnades, and close seigniorial woods,
    And the near ploughman whistling out his spells.
    We stand here tenderly, that painted shells
In the silverweed from us take no offence,
And mouse and rabbit come in confidence,
And if the tired leaf flutter anywhere,
It comes to rest on your sweet hand or hair.

If the sharp wind, that skimmed the sea just now,
Be kind at all, he's so, to kiss your brow,
And if those men who darkly in the past
    Broke flints and lit their fires and dug their ponds
Here—if those men are powers to bless or blast
    Steps that invade their homes and burial-mounds,

I think I feel them gazing mild on you
    As does the Unicorn, by legend true,
When, flaring up to charge deceitful man,
He sees a Virgin; he can smile, he can.

So now, the ghosts with black fierce heads grow kind
And wish you always here: Now you shall find
Our supper, coasting these warm furzes, these
    The Mushroom long has chosen for his haunt;
Under their eaves he crowds by companies
    And thinks of other fungi, lean and gaunt,
Unlucky ne'er-do-wells, that spring elsewhere.
So pride must have a fall; you have him there,
And there, and there; the stoic seems content,
For Sylva he perceives he by the stars was meant.

Well thought, old Mushroom; I in turn agree,
And add, this lady even was meant for me;
Whom now, for she's still hunting, I will seize
    And carry to some higher crow-perch yet,
And claim her kiss, and think, I crossed those seas,
    Dodged many deaths, and now at last have met
One who must be the vision and the crown
Of my best self, as now she is of this green Down.

THE BRANCH LINE

Professing loud energy, out of the junction departed
The branch-line engine. The small train rounded the bend
Watched by us pilgrims of summer, and most by me,—
Who had known this picture since first my travelling
        started,
And knew it as sadly pleasant, the usual end
Of singing returns to beloved simplicity.

194

The small train went from view behind the plantation,
Monotonous,—but there's a grace in monotony!
I felt its journey, I watched in imagination
Its brown smoke spun with sunshine wandering free
Past the great weir with its round flood-mirror beneath,
And where the magpie rises from orchard shadows,
And among the oasts, and like a rosy wreath
Mimicking children's flower-play in the meadows.

The thing so easy, so daily, of so small stature
Gave me another picture: of war's warped face
Where still the sun and the leaf and the lark praised Nature,
But no little engine bustled from place to place;
When summer succeeded summer, yet only ghosts
Or to-morrow's ghosts could venture hand or foot
In the track between the terrible telegraph-posts,—
The end of all things lying between the hut
Which lurked this side, and the shattered local train
That.
　　So easy it was; and should that come again—.

FROM AGE TO AGE

　　Retarded into history's marble eyes
　　Is their quick challenge and ability;
　　All the expression of their enterprise,
　　　The fierce, the rapt, the generous and the free.
Behold their monument; no more is now to see.

　　Travel this cool white day across this plain,
　　Count farms and haycocks, think of dead event,
　　Count all these graves, count every pang and pain
　　　Which put them here; but life will not relent.
Hardly the deathmask held one hour their last intent.

Action, eternal fire! from brain to brain,
From race to race, and age to age on-leaping,
Leaves the charred embers to the steady rain;
Over the skeleton the grass comes creeping,
And life's too short for wondering, too aflame for weeping.

TO ONE LONG DEAD

*Written on reading " Harriet," a novel by Elizabeth Jenkins, founded on
the Penge Murder of 1877. Harriet, who was a little " strange," had
some fortune. A scoundrel married her, got her money, and proceeded
with the co-operation of his mistress and others to imprison and kill
her and her baby by starvation.*

If any compact might be made
With those who rule time, chance and sense,
I'd purchase it with all I had,
And choose my moment cool and glad
To climb that stair and get thee thence.

Some sixty years, and fewer miles,
And some uninformation should
Be overcome; then like a flight
Of moonbeams instant, sure and right
I'd throng that room's cold stupid wood.

" Those? Those I no more understand
Than you; they are not of our kind.
They are not. Child, come forth, and bring
Thy child; if singing help thee, sing,
For we will hasten down the wind.

" Hungry wast thou? that pang is past;
And thy clammed body? now goes well;
Hast lost thy silks? here's more as fine;
Thy hair all knots? the gold lights shine
As ever before that darkness fell.

196

" The clouds of the east like tulips bloom
To bless thee forth; the moon in the west
Is lustrous with a joy in tears,
That thou hast slipt the barriers,
And bear'st thy boy on thy clear breast.

" Thou knew'st me when I came, didst thou,
That pitchy dark hid not my soul,
Nor thy quick smiling awaking, nor
The childlike artful conqueror
That thou went'st forth past that grim shoal.

" My name? I have no name, being only
Thy deep prayer come home to thee;
Thyself art all thou now need'st frame
For thy sweet thinkings; find a name
That grows in the grass or the apple-tree.

" And here's the place; thy wish, thy house,
Wide rooms prepared for him, for thee;
Thou hast desired and then denied—
Here taste, roam, grace thy eastertide,
Here dream, and waking, here thou'lt be."

If longings thus, like plans, can leap
Almost to that maimed Life, long stilled,
I hold some hope the Fates at length
As Beauty, Freedom, Faith and Strength
And Wisdom woke the unfrightened child.

A TOUCHSTONE

I think of Shelley, and my own poor speed
Becomes all glorious; mute till then, I sing;
His radiance is our modern angel's wing,
And if the choirs of heaven these days recede
Into bad silence, Shelley fills the sphere
    With anthems heavenly clear.

Granted the discords of his youth; the pace
Of youth's hot chariot is impolitic;
And his gray hairs at thirty show the race
Of man, that cannot quite teach God a trick.
Possessions too,—part fungus, and part flower,—
    Forced on him their half-power.

And grant his anguish of unmet desire,
" Shut out from Paradise "; O timely doom,
Before the round of days had robbed the bloom
From her he last believed a nature higher
Than all her kind! This said, look where he stands,
    And loose life's faded bands.

COUNTRY CONVERSATION

*The Council for the Preservation of Rural England has published Dr.
Vaughan Cornish's " Scenery of England," a volume which well sums
up the necessity for unspoiled natural scenery and solitude, and the
campaign for their maintenance.*

The Windmill: Well, I suppose I am soon to be dead and
    done for;
  I'm a cracked, crazy, idle thing; what do I face the Sun
    for?

I don't grind corn now, I don't swing my sails, and my
  smock's half gone,
And the boards down below say this is the place to put
  bungalows on.

The Lane: But what of me? I'm older than you; I'm a
  doomed thing too.
There's a rumour that says I'm a nuisance to motorists;
  probably true.
I'm only a zigzagging lane, with wild-rose borders,
And a few little birds in the bushes. I'm waiting for
  orders.

The Meadow: Waste not, want not. I fancied my chance
  in the days of my pride.
I brought the little children here, whole sunny days they
  wandered wide
Among my buttercups and mole-hills. I was their home.
But what of that? I'm to work. Promoted to Aero-
  drome.

The Spirit of England: Children, mistake not yourselves.
  Still glow to the morning;
Wind between mullein and primrose; accept May's
  adorning;
Deep your virtues. Life, not death, is yours,
Even as you are. Wisdom, vision this hour ensures
Through England from black Bolt Head to Hadrian's
  Wall
That you shall still abound in the noblest use of all.

IN A LIBRARY

A curious remedy for present cares,
And yet as near a good one as I know;
It is to scan the cares of long ago,
Which these brown bindings lodge.
                                    In black print glares
The Elizabethan preacher, heaping shame
On that iniquitous gay hell, the stage;
And here's another full of scriptural rage
Against high Rome. Fie, parson, be more tame.
This critic gnashes his laborious teeth
At that, whose subtlety seems no such matter;
This merchant bodes our economic death,
This envoy hastens with his hard-won chatter;
Age hacks at youth, youth paints the old town red—
And in the margin Doomsday rears his head.

AN OMINOUS VICTORIAN

I am the *Poems* of the late *Eliza Cook*,
For sixty odd years I have graced this nook;
I remember myself as a bright young book
    On a bookseller's ormolu table.

Just beside me I had quite a nice friend,
Mrs. Hemans's Works, and at the far end
Was one called *It's Never Too Late to Mend*,
    And a print of the Tower of Babel.

We were a pretty pair, *Mrs. H.* and I,
My crimson velvet was the best you could buy;
She wore green—and a love of a tie,—
    I suppose it would now look tawdry.

One fine morning she was taken, as I heard,
For a prize to a Miss Georgiana Bird.
Then my turn came—I'd to carry the word
　　Of " Podgers, with love to Audrey."

Some little time I was much in request,
Either she read me or hugged me to her breast,
And several sorts of ferns were pressed
　　Between my red-ruled pages.

O if only I could warn some of you young books,
Who are taken in like me by loving looks,
—There was no name then like *Eliza Cook's*;
　　It's preparedness that assuages.

Then, one night (I can almost see it still)
A letter came; she put down her quill,
And read, and stormed, " I should like to
　　That two-faced miscreant Podgers ";

And she flung me under the settee, where
I lay in want of light and air,
Enduring the supercilious stare
　　Of the *Works of Samuel Rogers*

That always stood on the bracket—well,
There's not much really left to tell,
I was rescued by the housemaid Nell
　　Who hadn't no time for reading,

But on the whatnot made me do
For a lamp (of the horridest butcher-blue)
To stand on; and she shrouded me, too,
　　In a mat of her mother's beading.

And here I am, and yet I suppose
I'd better not grumble, as this world goes,
For I see I'm outstaying rows and rows
    Of the newest immortal fiction;

And *Rogers* has vanished—I don't know where—
With his *Pleasures of Memory*—and I don't care;
I presume he's propping the leg of a chair
    With his sniffy elegant diction.

THE MARCH OF MIND

In ancient days, just before all that want of harmony
Between all right-minded people here and the others in
    Germany
I knew a sound tough farming kind of a man who played
    the accordion
But otherwise resembled very nearly that famous figure in
    Claudian,
The Peasant of Verona; he never roamed ten miles
Beyond his walks with a shotgun, and didn't wear out
    many stiles.
His greatest achievement was a tricycle, but it only appeared
Once or twice a season, because the horses thought it weird.
He did his work with considerable power, and he pulled
    the third bell,
And there were rum goings on in London's West End, as
    he had heard tell.
Now he can tell you a Delage is some car, and is really
    tireless
At appreciating Brahms and Economics " over the wire-
    less,"

Has been twice to the Strand Palace, rousing his third wife's
    suspicions,
And when he met me last offered to sell me four of my
    first editions.

ELEGY

ON HIS MAJESTY KING GEORGE V

To face the fortune of a scowling time,
    The omen and the rumour, we acclaimed
This quiet man proceeding in his prime;
    And his first triumph by foreboding maimed
Faded with little room for smile or sigh
When the world tempest plunged from that daemonic sky.

Recalling this, who does not picture still
    Silent battalions, those who first deployed
And met the lightning on the crest of the hill—
    Ironically went into the void?
Yet Irony, corporal of Valour, stood
Aside when two men's names arose, and called them good:

Kitchener dies not, his command endures;
    The King who heartened even that mighty heart
Stands with his marshal, and his gaze secures
    The dead battalions. These no more shall part.
With men like those, the Leaders and the Led,
Who can descant of hate? Who call their influence dead?

And who may school a kind? Might Machiavel
    Now from his table-book communicate
Precept or paradox that could do well
    In the nerve centres of a modern state?

Better the sailor's plainness; better still
The honest man's conviction, selflessness, good will.

An honest King's the noblest work of God—
    Now passes one whom all the world termed so.
Some terrified the highest with their nod,
    This Monarch held no subject high or low.
Whatever passion raged, it shall be known,
He but appeared or spoke: that storm was overblown.

Whatever Party claimed as right or wrong,
    That he was wise and kind offended none;
Therefore our love shall be his evensong;
    All dwellers in the dark and in the sun,
In the most populous, the most lonely places
Shall set a King among their old familiar faces.

LATE LIGHT

Come to me where the swelling wind assails the wood
        with a sea-like roar,
While the yellow west is still afire; come borne by the
        wind up the hillside track;
    There is quiet yet, and brightness more
    Than day's clear fountains to noon rayed back
        If you will come;
        If you will come, and against this fall
        Of leaves and light and what seemed time,
        Now changed to haste, against them all
        Glow, calm and young; O help me climb
        Above the entangling phantoms harrying
        Shaken ripeness, unsighted prime;
        Come unwithering and unvarying—

Tell claw-handed Decline to scrawl
A million menaces on the wall
For whom it will; while safe we two
Move where no knife-gust ever blew,
And no boughs crack, and no bells toll,
Through the tempest's ominous interval,
    Penitential low recall.

WRITING A SKETCH OF A FORGOTTEN POET

Here this great summer day,
    While the fields are wild
Wild flowers you name, I stay,
    And have learnedly compiled

From shaky books, too few,
    Dry registers,
Something of the living you;
    And have gleaned your verse.

You might have laughed to see,
    With this rich sun,
One pent in a library
    Who else might run

Free in the flashing sweet
    Life-lavishing air.
Or, lover of books, you'd greet
    Such constancy and care.

You might have laughed to hear
    Your stanzas read—
If it were not so clear
    The dead are dead.

What gulfs between us lie!
      I had thought them crossed,
   Dreaming to gratify
      Your unimpatient ghost.

AT CHRIST CHURCH, GREYFRIARS

In memory of Charles Lamb
who for seven years heard the Bible read every day there

Among all houses in haunted London
Behind whose windows we still perceive
Faces and passions of mortal genius
And, pausing, half rejoice, half grieve,
Is there one so kindly, one so lovely
As Christ's-house here with its constant dream
Of Christ-boys in their pretty myriads,
And one above all where he follows the gleam?

Here Time has served his mysterious Master
Much as in other matters: the race
Of boys are sped through youth and manhood.
Gone, "all are gone." But in this place
The impartial shadow has shown some weakness,
And seems inclined to hoard like toys
An aspect, an echo in gentle remembrance
Of numberless nameless blue-coat boys.

One above all, and Time still names him,
Has found Time's sergeantry less severe,
And holds his boyish world for ever
Singing and listening to music here,—
The music not solely of the musicians,
But of primal story, wisdom divine:
Here Lamb the child sits in rapture, the song being
Eden and Patmos and Adam's line.

Here in such form as the speech of England
Shapes how truly to deepest truth,
Elia in Tudor gown and girdle
Spies near as home the paths of Ruth,
The palace of Solomon, Job disastered,
Angels descending, fishers of men;
Thrilled with these visions, that fade in music,
Goes forth an enchanted citizen.

Come, child of elder fancy, man
Of child-like innocency; recall
The glances bright and voices of morning,
The opening paradise. Fair fall
The blessing on your lingering spirit,
And when no other is in the place,
We know that you, dear solitary,
Here see your Master face to face.

POETRY'S INVITATION

In happy hours, some hours, I spring;
From dense unhappiness I sing;
    I dance up like a meadow lark
Just where you thought there was never a thing.
I am not to be snared or trapped,
Spied out, astronomised or mapped,
And though you marked my last arising,
My next shall be as quick-surprising;
        Love me not—
        My love you have got;
        And hunt me fast—
        I flitted past;
I know no date, but where I play
It is perpetual proud to-day.

My wine is flashed in any cup
That takes my eye, flower-bell or pitcher;
Now some roisterer holds it up
And now the singing hedger and ditcher.
Told I more, you chance would dream
I meant to help you how to find me,—
Hear then: this my note, my gleam,
And there your wit, will, strength and scheme—
     Come, bind me!

AND THEN

Inconstancy, too rarely
   The theme of verse, a verse to you;
Some say you deal unfairly
   With human nerves; it is not true.
Lit by you and left by you I like my journey hitherto,
And still in a flash you may convince me I am waking
     long years since;
   I wish your sun, I wish your rain
   Dart elfish over the years that yet remain.

—This would be song for winds to sing
   If I knew all;
But while I listened the thrush took wing,
   The bell fell silent,
   My own footfall
Sounded alone, that face was gone
To whom I turned to make it known.
But still Inconstancy knows best, and the sudden turn of
     the lane is spring.

MINORITY REPORT

That you have given us others endless means
To modify the dreariness of living,
Machines which even change men to machines;
That you have been most honourable in giving;
That thanks to you we roar through space at speed
Past dreams of wisest science not long since,
And listen in to news we hardly need,
And rumours which might make Horatius wince,
Of modes of sudden death devised by you,
And promising protection against those—
All this and more I know, and what is due
Of praise would offer, couched more fitly in prose.
But such incompetence and such caprice
Clog human nature that, for all your kindness,
Some shun loud-speakers as uncertain peace,
And fear flood-lighting is a form of blindness;
The televisionary world to come,
The petrol-driven world already made,
Appear not to afford these types a crumb
Of comfort. You will win; be not dismayed.
Let those pursue their fantasy, and press
For obsolete illusion, let them seek
Mere moonlight in the last green loneliness;
Your van will be arriving there next week.

"CAN YOU REMEMBER?"

Yes, I still remember
The whole thing in a way;
Edge and exactitude
Depend on the day.

Of all that prodigious scene
  There seems scanty loss,
Though mists mainly float and screen
  Canal, spire and fosse;

Though commonly I fail to name
  That once obvious Hill,
And where we went and whence we came
  To be killed, or kill.

Those mists are spiritual
  And luminous-obscure,
Evolved of countless circumstance
  Of which I am sure;

Of which, at the instance
  Of sound, smell, change and stir,
New-old shapes for ever
  Intensely recur.

And some are sparkling, laughing, singing,
  Young, heroic, mild;
And some incurable, twisted,
  Shrieking, dumb, defiled.

VILLAGE SKETCH

Horses, their heads together under a tree;
Elm-trees and oaks, mantled in glistening green;
Streams silver-brimmed, the stream-divided lea,
Wide-rising ground with barley thronged or bean:
A town-end of good houses, something grave,
Gray, square, and windowing far; cypress and yew
Topping a long gray wall; five poplars wave
Above the dark-plumed wall; against high blue

Spear-flashing white the spire, and windcock new
Aloft the spire, proud plaything of these gales
Which bring more violet wreaths of cloud and swirl
Of whistling rain; the storm's great ghost assails
The boys with bat and ball, the blue-capped girl
Who leans with her young love against the pales;
While over the level the terrier speeds and springs,
Hoping to catch the swallows in their low swift rings.

CRICKET, I CONFESS

" Sir, I cannot profess to understand
One thing in England "—and Sakabé scanned
My face to be sure there was no offence astir,—
" It is Cricket, I confess. In the English character
That's the chief puzzle I have." " ' My horn is dry,'
If you don't understand it, no more do I."
Far out in the valley the sun was gilding green
Those meadows which in England most are seen,
Where churchyard, church, inn, forge and loft stand round
With cottages, and through the ages bound
The duckpond, and the stocks, and cricket-ground.
And I fell silent, while kind memories played
Bat and ball in the sunny past, not much dismayed
Why these things were, and why I liked them so.
O my Relf and Jessop and Hutchings long ago.

LONELY LOVE

I love to see those loving and beloved
Whom Nature seems to have spited; unattractive,
Unnoticeable people, whose dry track
No honey-drop of praise, or understanding,
Or bare acknowledgment that they existed,
Perhaps yet moistened. Still, they make their world.

She with her arm in his—O Fate, be kind,
Though late, be kind; let her have never cause
To live outside her dream, nor unadore
This underling in body, mind and type,
Nor part from him what makes her dwarfish form
Take grace and fortune, envy's antitone.

I saw where through the plain a river and road
Ran quietly, and asked no more event
Than sun and rain and wind, and night and day,
Two walking—from what cruel show escaped?
Deformity, defect of mind their portion.
But I forget the rest of that free day of mine,
And in what flowerful coils, what airy music
It led me there and on; those two I see
Who, loving, walking slowly, saw not me,
But shared with me the strangest happiness.

SIXPENCE TO THE RIVER

Some pause
To contemplate our Bridge because
Old *Camden* marked its stony strength
And marvellous length

When he declared BRITANNIA's pride;
Ben Jonson maybe at his side,
His pupil once but now his peer,
Admired the eloquent stream's career,
Promised a place to bridge and brook
In his forthcoming lyric book—
And maybe did not. I for one,
Though ready to break a lance for Ben,
Camden, Spenser and such sweet men,
Will stand to watch these ripples run
      And juggle the sun
On the stonework like a largess now
With quite unantiquarian brow,
With little of moralising wish—
      Unless, that fish
Were better used by men; and add
That by mysterious law each place
    Where Nature looks most gentle and glad
Attracts the rubbish-dumping race,
By whose refinement Nymph and Grace
    May walk in decent jam-jars clad.
But the gay water does its best,
Where vertebrae of traffic rest;
The currents seize each twisty chance
And dace in dozens thrill to the dance.
To-day I surmise should be some great
Day in the annals of our small state,—
Folks assemble; our splendid swans
Come bowing amid their myrmidons,
And where they ride the shining stream
A great perch glides with a champion's gleam;
The butcher's ducks masque like immortals
Trooping at crystal cloud-capped portals,
Never drake such sheen displayed—
It must be something more than trade.

And wildly hoping him to outdo,
Through the master arch the kingfisher flew
　　Ablaze in blue,
And back once more, a trifle vain
To be the escorting aeroplane;
Then someone rarer far than that
In broad daylight, a church-tower bat—
Once supposed black, but this gold light
And his circuitous sidelong flight
Bloom him as purple as tropic flowers;
There's a raree-show in this stream of ours,
And one old crow, town-crier elect,
From the elm recites what all expect.
So wait with me, on this warm wall,
For the climax of the festival,
First casting a silver sixpence in
To twinkle with ripple and feather and fin
And justify our presence here
Should the river god (and he must) appear.

DEPARTED

OR, 'TIS MORE THAN TWENTY YEARS SINCE

Moated and granged, recall the Gentry who
Could as they would, but never wrongly, do;
These at their wedding paid for anthem sung,
For voluntary played, and rice unflung.
Their funeral also had its golden tint,
Our choristers confused it with the Mint:
On the sad day, Regret would reign at three,
And later came Rejoicing with the fee.
To Gentry and no others was assigned
This special power: they in the evening dined.

Their cricket caps, of floral stripe and dye,
Proclaimed accomplishment, and did not lie.
For them a pitch smooth as their bowling-screen
Was guarded from the rougher, dustier green.
In church their knees impressed soft hassocks; they
At mattins came, at vespers were away,
Except that spinster whose kind cherubs flew
About her while she moved from pew to pew
Lighting the candles. Parrots, mourn your friend;
Canaries, let your trills to her ascend!

*　　*　　*

Who now succeed? What demigods have we?
Who scraped the gilding from the family tree?
Ask of the roadhouse, try the bungalow.
Welcome, Squire Thenks-Chum and Lord Arfamo.

STANZAS: MIDSUMMER, 1937

O England! lose not now, O never lose
　　The only glory that is worth endeavour;
The times are doubtful, and the task to choose
　　Desperately hard: but they have seemed so ever,
Men before now, staring into their age,
　　Finding it baffling, have proved masterful.
Be of their line; prepare for the turned page
　　Of outcome by the present scanned in full.

Reckon prosperity as a fleeting dance.
　　Grudge not adversity, for that unveils,
That counts the real wealth; yet if it chance
　　That England long advance with swelling sails,
Then be not proud; even Death, as English Donne

Interpreted long since, should not be proud;
Be unbeguiled. Measure not by the ton
   The wealth of nations. Mark each golden cloud.

How every country makes report of you,
   My country! with such attitude of praise
As Gibbon's Rome at high tide never knew.
   Envy herself but offers you the bays.
Speak then with love and knighthood of each fact
   Or project or desire of human good
In other nations; nothing thence detract.
   Be the true best by you best understood.

Too long, committed to such loyal course
   As even successful mummery claims from you,
You follow forms which must beget remorse.
   O England, cozened? Let old zeal renew.
If indolence were named a hanging crime,
   What thousands of us should be shortly sent
To execution! Mercy gives us time,
   And we may yet see what our cat-naps meant.

Arise then, and delight shall march with gain;
   Know what is honest, what is sly uncover.
Be what you have been; *English* is no stain;
   England has many an unexpected lover.
The clearness of the windows of the soul
   Men often sought and often found as yours.
Blue-eyed and lustrous, beautiful and whole,
   Prove now your bright Shakespearean sense endures!

IN THE MARGIN

While few men praise and hardly more defend
That armed power which from here, and as things are,
Appears the whole Japan; while this forced war
Inhuman drags to some inglorious end,
And kills, and fires, and fouls, I too must feel
Horror and wonder at the deeds thus done,
And fear each day's exploit of crashing steel
Has merely lost what old Japan had won.

But through the smoke and dust I still can see,
And may I not forget, much that belongs
To that great name "Japan" as well as those.
Faultless devotions raise clear eyes to me;
Through crowded streets gray-headed virtue goes,
And from poor farms I hear old peaceful songs.

THE HURRYING BROOK

With half a hundred sudden loops and coils
Between the limits of two humble farms,
Swerving and dodging like a boy who foils
His mates' pursuit; with numberless wild charms;
With beauty and joy my tiny river dances
The longest way he can, and prettiest too,
About our meadows, topped with shining lances
Of reed and rush, tunnelled in shadowy blue
Of thicket oak and alder and ivied shell
Of vast old willow; fast he runs and well
To keep his many appointments all at once,
Now the eel-stone, now the yellow lily, now the white,
Now where the fat vole on the clay ledge suns,
Here there and everywhere, a brilliant watersprite.

IN WEST FLANDERS

Is it the light that makes the silence
Of this long lake, for silence rules—
Though many row, or walk the terrace—
The curving shores, the china pools?
Or perhaps that hill of many memories
That citadels it high beyond
The farthest osiers, casts a spell
On this not quite coeval pond?

The air is populous with voices,
And yet the moment that we strayed
From the highroad, tempted by the cloister
Of elms towards the watery glade,
We were not conscious of these voices
But of a calm, a lull, a still
Invulnerable world of silence—
O quiet sky and lake and hill!

This sluice allows a bubbling current
To slide beneath the sluiceman's loft,
But that faint rumour lasts a moment
And unimaginably soft
Dies; and the gay and sly exchanges
Of parties in the boats aswim,
Out there among the lingering lilies,
Leave silence like an angel hymn.

What read you there, at your small table,
Young beauty with the varnished nails?
I read a—well—Victorian novel,
I seldom read such solemn tales,

But, finding it while I was waiting
For Albert (fishing over there),
I found I couldn't leave off reading—
I think it's something in the air.

And you, friend landlord, and chance comer,
Buying a view-card and a bock,
What are you worrying out together?
Nothing, we hope, that you will mock.
The fact is, he and I were talking
Of carp and how they seem to know
A friend who gives them bread or cherries—
They live a hundred years or so.

But quietly here, among these willows,
This boy has made himself a lair,
And we will question him in whispers:
He shines and warns us, "Please take care!
My friends the wood-mice suspect us,
I'm from the town—but here she comes,
The wisest and I think the mother
To carry off these dangerous crumbs."

Such notes upon the verge of silence
Imperil that deep flood no more
Than does the polished lessening ripple
Shaped by the angler's gentle oar;
The autumn evening now impending
Changes the painted lake we found,
But our enchantment travels on,
A silver silence of sweet sound.

TO W. O. AND HIS KIND

If even you, so able and so keen,
And master of the business you reported
Seem now almost as though you had never been,
And in your simple purpose nearly thwarted,
What hope is there? What harvest from those hours
Deliberately, and in the name of truth,
Endured by you? Your witness moves no Powers,
And younger youth resents your sentient youth.

You would have stayed me with some parable,
The grain of mustard seed, the boy that thrust
His arm into the leaking dike to quell
The North Sea's onrush. Would you were not dust.
With you I might invent, and make men try,
Some genuine shelter from this frantic sky.

VICTORIANS

Think not too glibly of their soft escape,
For if you do, the escapists you condemn
Will be yourselves; read first, and fully shape
The diagram of life which governed them.
I grant, these tall french windows, these smooth lawns,
These monuments announce their quiet years;
But who shall say what pale and anxious dawns
Smote these? Be certain ere you risk your sneers.
And of your charity admit that man
Need not for ever live in sharp distress;
Admit, that you as often as you can
Prefer to dance with happy thoughtlessness;

Devise some creed, and live it, beyond theirs,
Or I shall think you but their spendthrift heirs.

RHYMES ON BETHUNE, 1916

Old town of France, the wish to walk
Your friendly streets had been our talk
In roofless barns, in rat-run saps,
Among war's most heart-piercing shapes;
Our dead companions, they would speak
Of you, and smile, " Perhaps next week—
Perhaps next week I'll go on leave."
Faint visions, that did not deceive.
We, not struck down, dared not much think
Why all of us stood on the brink,
That should have been the safe highway
Towards Life's gardens sweet with May:
And not a man declined, Bethune,
Your most politely offered boon:
An art of life precise and keen,
Flowers on the table, *bonne cuisine*,
And, after nights in trench and keep
Sleepless, serene sweet-valanced sleep.
O that was blessing, that was luck,
Four miles from fire-steps, mines and muck,
To see a church not yet a wreck,
To enter the bank and cash a cheque;
And as my memory tells the tale,
No distance from the green canal,
From the inn window, still I see
My old platoon acclaiming me,
The old platoon, or some of them,
Enjoying life, which dolts condemn,

At the corner of a Rue whose name
They can't quite get, but like *quand même*;
They woo me to their kind retreat,
With song and joke and cognac neat.

　Leaving these boys I find my way
Where light winds in young lime-trees play
Along a pink but modest street,
While evening light falls sad and sweet.
Here I shall lodge, and here I find,
However critically inclined,
Two sisters, teachers, will not rest
Till they have lodged me " attë best,"—
As shy and gentle as wood doves these
Reveal their wish to set at ease
A scapegrace boy whose scanty French
Is all he brings from Auchy Trench.

　Why should I now so yearn to know
Just what they said, so long ago?
To put on canvas, pale and bright,
The countenances that smiled that night?
If only I could cause to flower
Afresh that happy vanished hour
When, hardly mentioning the great war
That ravined just beyond their door
These ladies stayed shamelessly late
In consultation and debate
With one outlandish, whom as guest
They welcomed to their timid nest!
I cannot *see* them now, I grieve
To fail in this. Let Time upheave
His oldest citadels: he can.
He hunts me out of all my plan.
But spite of him, if I may speak
As a not wholly cracked antique

In Paradise, I'll claim for these
Two ladies Learning's best Degrees,
And should exult did they in turn
Desire to see my cobwebbed urn.

WAR CEMETERY*

Why are they dead? Is Adam's seed so strong
That these bold lives cut down mean nothing lost?
Indeed, they would have died; ourselves ere long
Will take our turn. That cheque is signed and crossed.
But, though this dying business still concerns
The lot of us, there seems something amiss
When twenty million sudden funeral urns
Are called for. Have you no hypothesis?
Was heaven prepared for this abrupt incursion,
Was the word out to modernise the choir?
Or had the other congress (no aspersion)
A labour problem and a dwindling fire?
　In any case they're dead, and by their dates
　Nine-tenths should now be laughing with their mates.

No one can say they are not buried well,
At least as much of them as could be found;
Here grow abundant herbs of sweetest smell
And the rose here beats all; the easy sound
Of shears or scythe comes from the grassy border,
The blackbird runs across the shaven green.
Dressed by the right, fallen in with perfect order,
The dead contingents in gray stone are seen.

* No particular cemetery is alluded to. These stanzas were originally included
in the volume by several authors entitled *Challenge to Death*, published by
Messrs. Constable.

Some races cling to something more than stone;
" See, this was Georges, in his new uniform,
Bright cheeks, straight eyes—you really should have known
Our Georges." The photograph through sun and storm
  Lives its short life, says something that Georges said,
  But one still wonders why he should be dead.

Man, like some friends of his, is a grand fellow
For generous leaps into appalling holes;
Among his fears, the fear of seeming yellow
Urges him far, displaces, uncontrols.
Then he is prone to vanity, will dance
On steeple-points so he may end notorious,
And from his flowerful work will follow chance
Into the cannon's mouth to be called glorious.
But Georges arriving at the barracks felt
Fame rationed thin among so many clients—
Not many ways of wearing badge and belt,
Not many giants in a world of giants.
  I fear that Georges made some slight contribution
  To his untimely, unfair dissolution.

Blame him not much! O wish him what has brightened
Per saecula saeculorum Adam's race:
Life new-attained, limbs lissomed, conscience heightened,
The same old Georges with godhead in his face.
This for the present must be left mere wish,
And would have been the same if he had stayed
Along the streets of Calais hawking fish
Or where he was before the trumpets brayed.
There are whom I could blame with keener zest
Although his grave is such a garden now—
Vicarious heroes from whose mighty breast
Fumed the hot air that made those trumpets blow,
  Fishers of men with nets of strange device,
  Established in gold letters—at this price.

Ideals, after all, in noble states
Are necessary as the petrol pump;
While the great public slaves to pay its rates,
Someone must elevate the frowsy lump,
And from the rut of commonplace prosperity
Cry up adventurous passion, since elsewhere
Masked in most loathed fair-seeming of sincerity
Satanic synods, hand to hilt, prepare.
How sweet is power, one mind's command how sweet!
The patriot with his pencilled slips may feel
His headlines booming down the distant street
And shedding influence on each cottage meal.
    That Georges was gullible his chums admit,
    Or would, but have forgotten him and it.

Tyrtaeus led the way; the bards since him
Have done their best with martial strains to sunder
Georges, Hans, Bill, Carlos. Couched where goldfish swim,
They sing for glory: " There's a sound of thunder
Afar," to meet which tempest they approve
That every citizen should grasp a rifle,
In the direction of the thunder move,
Rush on the foe, transfix him. Death? a trifle.
Thus lyric genius ever stooped to cheer
The march that ends in billets under clay,
Melodious metres helped the lance and spear,
And should have stopped what came the other way.
    Love thou the poets. Georges even when he fell
    Had word from them: " See, what a lovely shell."

Is War so subtle, that of his machine
So meagre and absurd a wrack survives?
Or is Peace wise to clothe with such gay green
That spasmal visnomy whose menace thrives

The more, the less regarded or reported?
Assume which way you please, one thing is sure:
The face of Peace was hardly more distorted
By War's acids and axes than is War
Veiled from the sense of Peace. His metals die
Faster than skulls of those they struck to pieces;
A decade after, you may peer and pry
For strands of wire, for mortars whose caprices
    Made your days years, for shaft and iron emplacement.
    Vain search—to find inscrutable Effacement.

Perhaps the acres that have staged event
Will yield some whisper of it, might we hear.
Immense endeavour, tragic tournament,
History's smithying should not disappear
Without reverberation. Battle flames
With other ardours than of bursting shells,
And many a gray surviving soldier claims
That strange excitement surges nowhere else.
Walking past Mont Saint Jean I caught a drift
Of Waterloo's red crisis, and have known
Suspense and worse and felt the barrage lift
In even vaster battles of our own;
    Yet I have wandered stranger worlds than those,
    Planes which whoever dreams intensely knows.

Verbrandenmolen's windmill likes the breeze
That flies across this farmland; the bright toil
Is as it should be. Why alone are these
Condemned? But not these only, save we foil
The sails and cogs of other, uglier mills
Whose masters even keener wait each gust,
And beckon to false shapes of golden hills
Where Adam's seed may be ground down to dust.

Arise, young spirits, and march in pride, but not
Against your kind; attack at dawn, and capture
Line after line—but fire no single shot
Except of progress, and run through with rapture
   These old, gross demons: Rumour, Ignorance,
   Advantage, Spite, Conceit and False Romance.

That victory will be won, if I may trust
A thought that steals about this place, so mute
Upon what lately raged here. This poor dust
Ranked soldierly, these veterans salute
The promise; the old guard presenting arms
Trusts to the new, and gives it all it can.
Pointing at twinkling spires and big-barned farms
They smile a little. " As the thing began
It ended; only, as you see, we boys
Have copped unlucky, and the C.O. too,
But he'd just had *his* leave; well, all that noise,
And all us millions as they say *napu.*"
   Thus a dim music every step I tread
   Connotes the living purpose of these dead.

AFTER ANY OCCASION

   See what lovely hours you lost
While with a half-triumphant mind you crost
Lath-swords of words on some uncertain matter,
With dizzy-brilliant haste, with pompous thump and
    clatter,
In spite of which the rest enjoyed their private chatter!
       Think what quiet might have done,
       What simple watching would have won

Of human portraiture; how noble and how young
That profile of an ancient, keen as the line of hills
Beyond those sunset windows; hear how his silence fills
The hearts of those about him, hear, and hold your tongue.
Mark you too, how youth with bold emphatic error
    pleased
            At one stroke seized
This company; the willow-leaves on the tip of the tree no
    clearer
            Meet the sky.
I loved him for his scorn of the work that makes glad error
    die,
And how he lit the moment with his loyalty to a lie!
            So much the dearer.
But " store of ladies, whose bright eyes
Rain influence " all about you rise,
Whose crispéd hair, whose brows of calm, whose musical
    perfection might
Detain amazement for a thousand nights and one more
    night.
            But all are flown, and all are flown,
            And you may now grow wise alone.

A PASTORAL TO MADELINE

    In sunbright years
When, spite of Dr. Johnson on the way,
    Shepherds would play
On artful pipes and sing some roundelay
        To her who charmed that countryside,
    How I had tried the music to express
        Madeline's comeliness,
Bright-tressed, ready-smiling, April-eyed.

But now the shadows and north-easters strike
Along the vallies; kite and hawk and shrike
Are all our nightingaledom; shepherds stand
And with barbed wire and concrete mete the land,
  So flageolets are silent; yet shall she,
" My sprightly neighbour," have not a song from me?
    I will forgive her though she sticks
    To Madelinian politics,
And though she threaten me, grown quite a sheep,
With future lecture-tickets on that theme,
    Still, round the doorway I might peep,
    And love her for her earnest dream
Of betterment and liberal flocks and herds
        Happy as birds:
In my mind's eye, how fair her name appears
        In sunbright years!

TO THE EARL OF SURREY

" At £160 Mr. Edward Smith bought a 1585 edition of the ' Songs and Sonettes' composed by Henry Howard, Earl of Surrey, in 1537, when he was in confinement at Windsor Castle for having struck a fellow poetaster at Hampton Court. This was a late edition of a Tudor ' best-seller.' " Morning Paper, July 5th, 1938.

Illustrious poetaster, courteous lord
Of large estates, and (not the least) of verse,
We reckon you as nothing in the horde
Of clamorous bards, except that a long purse
Is still required to buy your cobwebbed book.
Sometimes a pallid student too may strive
To count your accents—some make four, some five
Per line, and annotate: " Surrey mistook. . . ."

My noble, valiant, eloquent Englishman,
Wyatt's comparable friend, fierce-beautiful,

See we are fallen on days which you not guessed,
Who led our language and our interest
Up shining ways, which should all Europe school,—
"Leaving great verse unto a little clan."

A NOT UNUSUAL CASE

It may be so: their love was never fire,
Never "a wonder and a wild desire,"
    What brought them first together?
        What "come hither"?
And what does that concern us now, or them?
Now, though life's whole vast various multitude
Were at their choice, and Venus wildly wooed
    With every stratagem,
        I still conclude
They would not alter much, nor dally far.
They, happiest in not following some queer star,
On usual roads, by frequent course, combined,
Are one, they mean one; them no tragic find,
Caprice, inversion, egotism shall break.
They are as children at the same good table,
Whom wisdom plenishes; whether bread or cake,
It is their common lot; not all are able
To count on daily sustenance; and this
Regular through long years is better bliss
Than chancing kickshaws. So, I guess, they live.
I wonder when it happened, their last kiss;
But maybe more than any kiss can give
Dwells in their composition: smile who will,
They thread the maze that baffles beauty still.

THE SUM OF ALL

So rise, enchanting haunting faithful
Music of life recalled and now revealing
Unity; now discerned beyond
Fear, obscureness, casualty,
Exhaustion, shame and wreck,
As what was best,
As what was deeply well designed.
So rise, as a clear hill road with steady ascension,
Issuing from drifted outskirts, huddled houses,
Casual inns where guests may enter and wait
Many a moment till the hostess find them;
Thence ever before the carter, passing the quarries,
The griffin-headed gateways,
Windmill, splashing rill, derelict sheepfold,
Tower of a thousand years—
Through the pinewoods,
Where warm stones lodge the rose-leaf butterfly;
Crossing the artillery ranges whose fierce signs
Mean nothing now, whose gougings look like
Bird-baths now; and last, the frontier farm
And guard-house made of bracken.
Rising to this old eyrie, quietly forsaken,
You bear me on, and not me only.
All difference sheds away,
All shrivelling of the sense, anxious prolepsis,
Injury, staring suspicion,
Fades into pure and wise advance.
So rise; so let me pass.

THE HOME OF POETRY

Willing to give whatever art I know
To some new theme or old one newly springing,
I hear fresh hours appeal, I mark the flow
Of daring wits; they promise well. I go
     Where older friends are singing.

It is not mine to choose; the deeper call
Is master yet. The child is that they made him.
His eyes, his voice, his mien and walk are all
Out of his jurisdiction. Life arrayed him,
     And life will weave his pall.

A thousand ways I travelled, and I heard
A thousand ways of reasoning and regarding;
And sometime hoped to find some thought and word
Which might swell my estate—a hope deferred,
     Now noted for discarding.

So mighty is the motherhood of sense,
The poetry of time before the yearning
For poetry took form! The narrow fence
Of first things is song's liberty. Returning,
     I hail magnificence.

TO TEISE, A STREAM IN KENT

Watersprite whose voice and look
Unique and multitudinous took
My childish fancy, at first glance
How clear the difference of your dance.

I could no more confuse your style
With Beult who flowed in the next green mile
Than take our smith or carrier for
Our saddler. Now, one plaudit more
For you, my strange familiar friend
And one deep prayer. May no man end
With short-seen plan or powerful greed
The centuries of your joy; may reed,
Osier, pollard, alder, thorn
And oak defend you night and morn,
And cattle in your lily-pool
With sad stare shame away misrule.
May kingfishers like flames attack
Dullness and send him wiser back,
Squadrons of gem-eyed hobby-horses
Whirr round his iron-minded forces;
And do you then, gentle stream,
Assume your wintriest wild extreme,
And (as I have known amazed) pour down
Among your goblin willows brown
Deep-dooming floods and foaming flocks
Of whirlwaves till the midnight rocks
With what you say to those who dare
Affront you with some coarse affair.

TRIUMPH OF AUTUMN

I see your signal, and the lands have seen,
And are prepared. Your hour, your fortune. Ride
More boldly then where none can intervene,
Not now in some pale bough or low mist hide.
With conquest occupy your splendid scene,
Throng the fantastic tourneyings of your pride.

233

Your hour, your fortune. Undisguise your will
And try your genius, king, from bannered grove to golden
        hill.

        Vast is the triumph which at your behest
        Will blaze abroad. The sun himself shall stride
        With clanging pomp, bronze east to rubied west,
        The moon sway wine-flushed after, lion-eyed
        Star-companies form, tree-columns of glittering crest
        Uphold their rank in blue air, strong and wide
        Rivers go wheeling through enormous plains,
Forests assume the purple, harvests roll their rumbling
        wains.

        Meanwhile let no one whisper time's plain fact,
        Or hint an embered ending. Leaves that sighed
        In falling syllabled no wrath. The stacked
        And vatted yield of the year has not denied
        This cloth of gold. The church clock told exact
        Moment on moment gone, but only plied
        His task in the general show and with gilt hand
Paid compliment, meant nothing but a child may under-
        stand.

        Who cannot now be glad with even the least
        Of the pageant? Here the pear tree warped and dried,
        There cob suspected barren, brings brave feast,
        Bright apples lantern the earlier eventide.
        With elder, hop, crab, blackberry, sloe increased
        To swell your flame each straggling hedge has tried,
        Great season; sunflowers clamber atop each fence,
Flaring salute, each aster like his master beams immense.

        These in the margin of the world-wide page
        Whereof you paint the midst, these orbed and pied

Delay the eye that you would wholly engage
With your own sanguine colours. Light airs glide
About your streamered car, your travelling cage.
They were but perfume wafting, and they died.
But some tell me they hear them gathering power
Until with ocean voice they sound the extinction of your
      hour.

A PROSPECT OF SWANS

Walking the river way to change our note
From the hard season and from harder care,
    Marvelling we found the swans,
The swans on sullen swollen dykes afloat
Or moored on tussocks, a full company there,
White breasts and necks, advance and poise and stir
Filling the scene, while rays of steel and bronze
From the far dying sun touched the dead reeds.

So easy was the manner of each one,
So sure and wise the course of all their needs,
So free their unity, in that level sun
And floodland tipped with sedge and osiery,
It might have been where man was yet to be,
Some mere where none but swans were ever kings,
Where gulls might hunt, a wide flight in from sea,
And page-like small birds come: all innocent wings.

O picture of some first divine intent,
O young world which perhaps was modelled thus,
    Where even hard winter meant
No disproportion, hopeless hungers none, '
And set no task which could not well be done.

Now this primeval pattern gleamed at us
Right near the town's black smoke-towers and the roar
Of trains bearing the sons of man to war.

THE NAMELESS STREAM

I wonder not the Poets love the brooks
And throughout life seek their society;
I think there's scarcely one of their rich books
But has its stream that runs there merrily,
And plays as young as when their lives were new,
As musical as first it bade them hear,
Forget-me-nots in the banks as tender blue
As when their child loves chose them without fear.

Of all things young the reverence is not hard;
It goes through nature, its own beauty smiles
Wherever life sets forth with brows unscarred
Singing its journey to enchanted isles.
Of all things young the brooks are not loved least,
So sparkling from their birth and dancing so;
Their happy solitude has never ceased
To call the wise to wander where they flow.

Now in the bluebell wood in cool clefts poured
They brim their ivy-tangled pools and now
Wind into shallows parting pasture sward
And much they please the sun-teased horse and cow,
And spread white sands, and build up pebbly lairs
For loach and bullhead, while the flitting wren
Comes to live with them, and the kingfishers;
And labourers bless them, and poetic men.

THOUGHTS OF THOMAS HARDY

" Are you looking for someone, you who come pattering
Along this empty corridor, dead leaf, to my door,
And before I had noticed that leaves were now dying? "

    " No, nobody; but the way was open.
    The wind blew that way.
    There was no other way.
    And why your question? "

" O, I felt I saw someone with forehead bent downward
At the sound of your coming,
And he in that sound
Looked aware of a vaster threne of decline,
And considering a law of all life.
Yet he lingered, one lovingly regarding
Your particular fate and experience, poor leaf."

GIBBON: IN THE MARGIN

    What would I give to have been
    With Gibbon when first in great preview
While the barefooted friars were chanting their vespers
    He gained his entire scene
Of imperial passions, contentions, illusions.
    And out of them simply drew
    The future's picture, man at last
    Grown safe, schooled out of his perilous past?

    What would I give to be
    With some new Gibbon when all his thought
Over nations in throes and the springs of their quarrels
    Perceives on a sudden the key

To the riddle, and comes to the multitude speaking
 In honour and welcome? New-wrought
 His engine of peace, I see him strong,
 And the world amazed it had waited so long.

TO THE MEMORY OF COLERIDGE

Moonlight and water mist
 Like visions from your Ballad haunt the night,
 And constellations burn above dark towers.
 Alone at length
 I come to you, my friend from boyhood hours,
 My Grecian, test of truth and tower of strength,
 With great desire to tell you how your light
Streams from your cottage window, blow wind as it list.

Time's face with shadows red
 Of doubt and error, rage and grudge lours still.
 I turn to you, Ulysses of your day
 Whose view comprised
 So many times and nations, whose survey
 Made seers of those who heard you: thence advised
 I catch beyond the transient chaos shrill
The music of a mind which yet moves well ahead.

Your faith, which casual wit
 Follows not far, compact of lore and love,
 Of near or distant image, gleams and yields
 A promise now;
 And through the moonlight, in our towns and fields,
 Yearn the immortals. Once again the vow
 Is made to them, pagan and Christian move
For the soul's health, and as in your wide world unite.

At this you frown; I hide
My face a moment, if therein I err,
And am content to stay where last you pointed—
    These English shrines
Beneath high elms best house the Lord's anointed,
And the Triune you loved there loveliest shines.
In fields you said that natural altars were,
But for the perfect godhead stood at Herbert's side.

    Had our time-tracks combined,
Much had I moved you to that gracious gift,
Which crowned the rest; you had raised more dream-
        towers with
        Your far-sweet song;
You whose young fairy-secret is my myth,
Whose pilotage is safe through seas of wrong,
Whose years of joy and pain finally lift
Over the age the timeless house of singing mind.

LASCELLES ABERCROMBIE

It was not mine to know your younger strength,
But from your words I caught some charming sense
Of the glad lyrist now in orchards walking,
Now on high moors, and always friend of morning,
Curious and happy in the rural round.
Great was your wisdom in all kinds of learning,
As though you could have lectured to Longinus,
Or taken a flail with Clare, or sailed with Shelley,
And tuned Æolian harps or mended millwheels,
Or founded bells or run a raree-show.
Modesty never beaten ruled your talk
Of that great art which through all usual tasks

Lived in you; serious-sweet you guarded that
From casual comment and from personal aim,
Still meditating what the masters wrote
And building temples to the Muse apart.
I feared not your untimely vanishing,
I thought you had before you still a calm
Chaucerian age, and every witty glance,
Clear recollection, dry reflection proved it.
So lost! yet the brief season of our meetings
Is on my life most graciously inscribed.

THE TWO BOOKS

Come tell me: of these two books lying here,
Which most moves heart and mind to tenderness,
The one approaching its three-hundredth year,
The other a recruit fresh from the press?
The one well honoured down the years, and still
Trusty to light our pathway, poise our view,
And this as yet uncrowned, which may fulfil
As great a task through centuries strange and new?
In both you find one nature, one appeal,
And that antiquity and this young birth
Share the same glory, equally reveal
Man in his wisest, luckiest hours on earth.
Man the inventive with his ceaseless power
Of shaping engine, fabric, instrument,
Never wrought better than in the early hour
Which gave him books; and to his short span lent
Almost eternity, to his local speech
Almost unbounded range. Thus from the tomb
Unseen romancers charm, apostles teach,
The white truths conquer and the kind loves bloom.

A world so opens on us by this key,
We may not count its continents; we may glide
Over a myriad-times extended sea
And land of life abundant, time denied.
And this, like roses in the year's decline,
This blest invention grows much sweeter now,
And while the rest is shadow this will shine,
Invincible amid great overthrow;
So speak and mean these two books lying here,
And differing as may be, alike grow dear.

TRAVELLERS, 193-

Bright insolent winds assail the shores
    Of northern France, and the crested waves
Tilt at the miles of sands and shingles
    Where as yet no public misbehaves.

Pale painters get a trifle busy
    On the shut kiosks and blank cafés,
But as yet there's more suspicion than hurry
    And the wind will pound yet several days.

Wild scampering sunbeams show the city
    Is clamorous red and silver blue,
And straight-lined fortifications yield
    Part shelter, whence that coloured view.

Strong-elbowed and with wondrous beard,
    Whose statue's this? read who it is, Clare;
Who, I'll forget inside ten minutes,
    And I'll not forget you reading it there.

I wonder, I, the older traveller,
   What you and John are taking back,—
Nothing maybe of my perceptions;
   A different series, another tack.

The wind may sing his sea-song later
   In your review as he will in mine,
The coast of England gloom and glitter
   To you as to me: so the moment shine,

It will be enough, for watching you meeting
   With foreheads smooth this sharp clean day,
I feel at once deep joy and trouble,
   And winds glowing each a separate way.

THE VANISHING LAND

Flashing far, tolling sweet, telling of a city fine
The steeple cons the country round, and signals farm and
      kiln and mine,
Inns by the road are each one good, the carters here are
      friendly men,
And this is a country where I mean to come again and
      come again.
There was a child, though, last time I was passing by St.
      Hubert shrine,
A child whose torn black frock and thin white cheek in
      memory brighter shine
Than abeles and than spires. I said, I pledge this blossom's
      better growth,
And so began, but one day failed; what sightless hours, and
      busy sloth

Followed, and now the child is lost, and no voice comes on
    any wind;
The silver spire gets farther off, and the inns are difficult to
    find.

THE VICTOR

O lightening love that makes drab lanes
    Bright avenues to joy's high way,
And forth from black-souled hurricanes
    Conjures glad day!

O limitless love that he and she
    Find winged for worlds in one embrace;
That under one small roof or tree
    Commands all space!

O living love in whose great birth
    Death counts for nothing, proved a lie,
Still blaze and blossom through old earth,
    And sea and sky.

FULFILMENT

Fulfilment is a puzzling goddess,
    And though her jewelled shrine
Is so magnetic, we may tarry
    And ask, Is she divine?

But if the answer be, No question,
    Still let us spend our gift
Of time on pilgrimage together,
    And watch the lazy drift

243

Of autumn leaves in casual currents
    Towards the new-found weir,
And count the unimpassioned willows
    And dreamless palings here;

And pass the corporal with his sweetheart,
    And happily dissent
Over the hue poured in the waters
    From the modern tenement

Which ventures nearly to our river;
    Its blue-frocked children play
Carelessly there where Nature played with
    Solitude yesterday.

And I, concerned to see the picture,
    Suspect Fulfilment wins;
Wherever we had forecast her chapel,
    Here her reign begins.

There was a hope—but I have forgotten,
    For now is hope fulfilled;
And, watching your bright brow this moment,
    I have no house to build.

THE FLOWERS

They fade then; other flowers have faded,
And these were flowers.
Had I been watching closer or less jaded,
They should have lived yet some sweet hours.

But in their spent bloom I discover
Not care alone,
But what live truth it is to be your lover,
And know you make my course your own.

244

Bringer of flowers! and friend of failings,
Young and brave love,
I count these wraiths as my own unavailings,
And yet my thoughts towards you in glory move.

THE WATERFALL

I haunt a waterfall
Not so tall
Measured by mapcraft, but to me
None is there through this world to see
From mightiest peak or blue rock wall
Like this fair fall.

I haunt a waterfall,—
So I call
These flowing shining locks set free
Whereamid a spirit of Nature she
With eyes of love looks forth to enthral;
Whom fair and fair befall.

TIME TOGETHER

When you are by, I think of time as boys
Set forth on brave excursions in the spring,
Which opens the green landscape and long hours;
I am all contentment, never a presage lours
On my delicious pastures; the blue ring
Of heaven perhaps I mark, beyond my joys;
But that's too far for fear; if that be all,
Why, I can say there's room, no fence obtrudes nor wall.

Such is your well-tuned, wild-flowered, world-bright
    grace,
Giving me sense of wide free ways, so free
And wide that I count nothing of time and space,
But think these present gifts will ever be;
Childlike the bliss, and childlike too dismayed
I find the moment come which ends our endless glade.

CLAIRE'S BIRTHDAY IN 1940

This is your day, but can this be your year?
What likeness bears this angry turbid stream
Of months with one hoarse theme
To your long love of life and welcome clear
For all that wars not, growing in its place,—
What has this curse to do with your embrace?

Yet for your birthday let us make our rhyme,
Wishing old Chaucer near to do it right,
Who would have hailed your light
And sent your legend far beyond a time
Of passions armed with horror and hell-pride,
And shown your fineness as the future's bride.

Royally would he have sung, since he had skill
In portraiture of ladies' loveliness,
What I can only bless:
The happy beauty dawning brighter still
Each day from noble forehead, fearless eyes,
Lips where with wit deep understanding vies.

THE SPRING GALE

Sound, sound, immortal Tempest, through the dark,
Set a pent heart, a captive wild-bird free,
For I have One who passes every mark
To run and rise and round the world with thee.
And she is timeless, unenslaved is she,
The spring's great impulse all the year indwelling
In her warm breast, and tirelessly excelling
The dust of dry extinction: Sound in tree
And arch and reed, for there will my Love be,
Of all the Venus and the vital spark;
And, herald, conqueror, epitome
Of sharp and sweet begetment, only agree
That thou as she art gentle; dawn shall hark
With me to your one song from the heaven-beseeching
    lark.

ONE AMONG THE ROSES

While by the rosebed gay you stood, and revelled in the
    multitude
Of blooms with unfamiliar names, and tints and folds new-
    found, new-sweet,
We wondered much at the rich power which breeds so
    many and many a flower
Not like the myriads known before, and each one lovely
    and complete.

And while you touched the leaves and bowed your bright
    head there among the crowd,
Murmuring of roses you would have in the small garden
    of your dream,

I wondered much at the great grace which fashioned your
  clear rosy face,
After the myriads gone before, a beauty new and now
  supreme.

THOMASINE

No stranger yet no friendlier call
      Ever did befall
Young clear-spoken Thomasine
On all the errands she had been
By chapel, covert, warren, hall
Than that vast evening floodlit far
With the sun gone down, so calm, so clear.

It was little enough, save there and then.
The moorcock crowed and called his hen
A distance off in a pool unseen
Of that quicksilver, that sharp green
Beyond the mill and weir,
All so clear,
All so secret; again the cry
Climbing the miles and miles of sky.

Here some wood stacked, there a van,
A slated sty, a rusty can,
A notched millstone, a pumiced step,
A walnut tree and a bee-skep.
The miller's house, that stares at distant land.
She had him thenceforth in her hand;
She knocked, he came; it might have been planned;
But her thought was up the stream—
That call in the reeds was all her theme.

" This I should read at once—forgive me;
Child, come in, and kindly give me
A moment or two to think it over."
Thomasine, scan well your lover.
All past guesses, all your glancings,
Preferences and fragile advancings,
Flown with the last of the snowflakes, see you?
But his plain business waits not—be you
Gone to your dad with the answer now.

Who shall determine how
She and he, thus met on a rarish
Journey into the bounds of the parish,
Meet and meet? Life's many-roomed
Mansion has but one room for them now,
He would kiss her mantle's hem now,
Only now known; and she has bloomed.

The afterglow, a wild-bird's voice,
A sound of sluices, could these make
A charm which lured her to her choice,
And gave her subtle strength to take
Like any witch? I dare not screen
My thought from the chance that just this one
Reed-note from beyond the world else known
Woke a new song in sauntering Thomasine.

See, she comes, she dances it down
The furze-hill lane by the sandpit brown;
She can count the way by grains of sand,
She knocks, and has him in her hand.
And he, straight worker, not the worst
Of heirs, not catching her at first,
Is now alive to her alive,
And blue night falls. The splashing rills

Over the deep-dropt penstocks dive,
The trout's leap trills
And the waters resound in a round.

" Finish the day, pack those away,
Those tiresome papers,"—he complies,
And still she leads. " I hear you play."
The music challenges. While it dies,
She from some lovely distance cries
A note she learned; he must obey.
Can this, she asks, be Thomasine?
Can ever such dear love have been?

They are talking trouble, along the street,
Talking Wicked, Indiscreet,—
Few will be pleased, but gods are pleased
When love comes flying for love once more.
Most forget, some never heard
That simple and mysterious word
That came to Thomasine, who knew.
Nature tried and found her true.
She told this to a friend, who smiled
Sadly at things so silly and wild.

The primrose here I'd happily bring
To peep with grace, the wren to sing;
The thrush's egg I'd borrow to deck
This chronicle with a hue as pure
As it should have; the royal swan's white neck
Should not the shining whiteness there one whit
      obscure.
" Love, I was nothing till you made me Me."
" And I was here alone, and here are We."
Thence in its strength their epithalamy.
The mirror gleams in the shades, the ancient house
Whispers of something known to the apple-boughs

Just by the window; she, a thought alone,
Listens to all the night, comes, claims her own.
All the hosts of fear are nothing here,
Grudge and bad cheer
Overthrown.
He does her no wrong; she wins him, she the flood
That bears him childlike, while he thinks his voyage
    good.

Day, and life ahead;
Would it were mine to utter more
Than from some broken knowledge now was said.
And trace them in Time's wonder, shore on shore
Achieving; only trust we this,
Under our harsh world wells such constant bliss.
Blessed it is, and when it upsprings through,
Its beauty assoils the worst that hate can do.
Blessed that sign of venture given, that chime
From solitude when reeds are green,
And answered as by Thomasine
Through the tangles of chance and time.

THE WINTER WALK

Now while the winter wind at last,
    As angered by delay,
Hurls all he has of shrewd or vast
    To pound the world to clay;

While brown woods slant and sing his hymn
    With roaring voice, and shed
Here droves of leaves and there a limb,
    And look like witch-worked dead;

I walk alone, and walking so
　　As ever find you there,
And talk with you, and boldly go
　　Through all this rush and tear

As if it were the calmest place
　　And moment, and as though
That sunshaft lit fair Nature's face
　　With all the flowers that blow.

And off it flies, and leaves the plain
　　In desolate dying need,
Where from the shapes of summer's reign,
　　The latest born, recede.

Once more they humbly sink away,
　　Their little lives resigned
Might scarcely want this tempest day
　　To cut them from God's mind.

And I who pass much like the sere
　　And outcast leaves and straws
Must think on all that disappear
　　By these inclement laws;

The more because my mind is bent
　　On brightest souls, on one
Who seemed for ever-living meant,
　　For an age of song and sun.

And you with me, well-loving long
　　That mortal, smiling sigh—
As sweet and sad as his best song—
　　" But even I shall die."

I have no thoughts, nor could have words,
 Nor will I yet believe—
I look away to feeding herds
 Who kindly might deceive.

Their honest heads, their lusty sides,
 Their haltless pasturing claim
That, whatever airy demon rides,
 They find the world the same;

And look, those birds with perfect ease,
 Proud-crested, not a care
From the black north unsteadies these:
 They have all time to spare.

Fine-drawn illusion! still my heart
 Chills with the truth I know,
That all created joy must part
 And the very brightest go:

A river wider than all sense
 Of measure, whose skull-waves
Are all whom winter hustled hence,
 Whose eddies are the graves

Of million millions, glorious grown,
 Then of no interest,
This river all too clearly known
 Comes flooding through the breast.

" O heart," I hear you say, and feel
 Your warm hand on my hand,
" Be peaceful, let the storm of steel
 Rush timely through the land

Without the cohort of your dreams,
    Unless such dreams as bring
Me to your arms; your lethe-streams
    Will vanish at the spring."

They vanish now; I hear no storm,
    I fear none; you are spring,
The golden meadows western-warm
    Around us flower and sing,

And if eternal be, its light
    Is upon our now, our here,
While you cast Maydays on Time's night,
    My beautiful and dear.

GOD'S TIME

A gentler heaven steals over the hour,
    And at its pace I go
    And scan green things that grow
Beneath old hedge and ivy-bower.
Most gracious falls the silent hour.

Through the shut sky an eye of blue
    Twinkles upon the soul,
    Even as these weeds unroll
Their leaves aspiring, choice and new;
    Their greenness blesses, and that blue.

The round leaf, shield leaf, patterned spray
    All shine like love's first tears,
    And though no primrose peers,
Nor aconites, nor windflowers play,
I have their message through leaf and spray.

This may not be the hour I supposed
        When from the house I came
        Informed of a world aflame;
That will have been an era closed,
Though endless as I then supposed.

O green leaves born in winter's heart,
        White ghosts of flowers to be,
        Come here so quietly,
And blossoming heaven's blue counterpart,
—I have lost my way, and found my heart.

AT A CATHEDRAL SERVICE

"The almond will soon be flowering," said she
With Nature's smile on her lip, in her eye,
"Though here there may be no almond tree,
But I feel it so." The New Year sky
Was shining on the Cathedral then,
"I hope the sun shines through the windows," she said,
And into matins we went once again,
In peace and love and thankfulness wed.

Through the windows tall and white the sun
Shone well, and his rays blest the simple hour,
Touched the cheeks of the children, and haloed one
White effigy, made the almond flower
In my Love's mood, while the trees in the wind
With light dancing branches beyond the glass
Seemed to have buds they dreamed to unbind,
To reach beyond months of steel and brass.

The voice of the prophet so often read
Was new again and the vision new,
And said to my depths what my dear had said;
The singing of the boys resounded it too.
We wished that the world might all be won
By the chime and colour the moment wove,
The almond blossom of spirit, the sun
Of diviner fires, and eternal love.

HALF A CENTURY

Sweet this morning incense, kind
    This flood of sun and sound of bees;
Now what a heavenly day to find
    The new-born white anemones
    Among old Medway's willow-trees.
    Out then at once, and cross the leas,
Go swift as light through miles of green,
—There never were such flowers as these!—
    And sing as sings the bird,—Begone;
    The church-clock bell gives warning, On,
    There far ahead fly swan and swan!

But fifty years have come between.

NATURE'S BEAUTY

DURING A CRISIS OF WAR

Dream-like the little journey in the sun,—
The path, first, where the hop-plants had begun
To reach for their fresh twine as if they knew
(And through their old succession doubtless do:)

256

From this trim garden, much as one borne on
By some delightful vigour not his own,
I found my fortunate uncharted way,
Splendid with April's high-triumphal day.

Yet I could scarcely feel so much the light,
The eager earth, the brown farm just in sight,
The farmer steering out his field machine,
As something less disclosed. This might have been
Another country! When the hedge mouse stirred
From root to root, or when the wild bee whirred
Sharp by the bee-fly poised above the stile,
The whole thing lived in subtlety awhile;
And all the flowers where farther solitude
Received me wandering, played some interlude
Upon the accustomed scene but not of it,
As though indulged for their old favourite
To come, how long? Yet flowers well known were these,
Violet and primrose, daisies, anemones,
Wood-strawberry-cup, starflower and celandine.
None overhead but what we all have seen,
Blackthorn begemmed, crab-apple's rosy drops,
Wild cherry the white lady of the copse.
In all they made Spring's old familiar tale,
They, and crescendos of the nightingale,
And the wren's twittering, and, the morning through,
Calls of the now monotonous cuckoo.

All hovered as a dream for my regard.
The other-country gods were watching hard.
The loveliness and liberty stayed theirs,
—Mine, swift recall. I passed as he who bears
But a brief-dated leave, and in this age
Scarcely to be acquired. The radiant page

So gently shown, so firmly turned, might seem
Of earth's and man's book once; this day, a dream.
So shown, so turned, the fairy writ was gone,
And only a pretty mist, unmeaning, lingered on.

NATURE'S ADORNINGS

Whence is such glory? who would know
The slough and swamp could yield it? Forth it leaps
Above the wreck of woods, where no path is,
Illuminate, yellow flag in flower, true prince
Of desolate places. If a child pass here,
Whose dreams have grown unhappy with the ghost
Of this feared swamp, immediately the flame
Of courage in green stem and golden wreath
Shall break that spell.

The splendours of the world
Are such that number and inquiry fade;
There is no reason for them but themselves,
That they are such, is felt as wonderful
Compared with what they grow from; so it is.

The child soul-struck with the yellow flag's new fire
In the next moment sees his kingfisher,
Than stained glass brighter, all his bravery on,
Of all our small birds only so adorned,
A tense blue instant; and this sumptuousness—
To haunt a tiny trampled pasture brook.

In that same brook, though, several splendours live;
The perch, a champion armed and blazing, scorning
The common shoal, empurples the gray sands.

What flawless lustrous life the swan's breast sheds
In subtler shinings on the gazing child;
And then, mocking the other panoplies,
The dragon-fly zooms round, a diamond nerve.

On him and them the summer's frown will fall,
And cloud their jewels with ereboean gloom,
Thunder's slow heavy nihilistic wave.
Thence, even thence, the glory springs in swift
Splendour of iris'd lightning; thus once more
The slough and swamp of nature yields this wild
Royal extravagance, this conquering pride
In singular blazonry, to witch the world.

BUTTERFLY DANCE

Among the rest, four butterflies,
Together met, flew here and there
As if one will said " Swerve " or " Rise,"
" Fan these tall flowers," " Ascend in air,"—
And wildly happy, fleet and sure
From weed to wheat flew that light four,
The admiration of a boy
Who stood and caught their choric joy.

A harvest sun imbrowned the plains
And thistle-waifs sailed with the whims
Of invisible breezes, the green limbs
Of bindweed wound their wilful chains
About the loosestrife and the bean,—
And round about, above, between,
That fluttering, twinkling four was seen;
What secret might such oneness mean?

Seemed the glad frolic would last for ever—
Nothing to shadow their hearts or sever;
Now their snow-white turned rich blue,
Caught from the sky,—or given thereto?
There, they must surely drift apart,
But they did not, all as one athwart
Zigzagging; now more slowly all
Almost into the white-cups fall.

And so at unity these four then
Appeared, it was more wonder when
One of them from the enchantment broke
And in a breath was over the oak
And came no more; soon then the rest
Chose several air-ways, east and west,
A symbol which the boy one day
Would find too true for friendships flown away,

THE BOY ON THE WAGGON

With what delight the south's large rain
Came singing down, came too the gale
And turned the leafy poplars pale,
And rippled miles across the grain;
Such rain and wind were what he loved.
The boy who on the farm-cart sat
With one white sack for coat and hat;
The scents of summer roved
With bees and swallows through the gusty shower,
Round this country boy in flower,
And while he called his lazy mare
To keep a-moving, fair and fair
    The picture in his mind.

" I love her, boy, I hardly know
What I can say, buy, do to show
Marie that she is more to me
Than the rain and the wind could ever be,
And, let our beanfield do its best
To flood the world with deep sweet zest,
Let skylarks mingle music-showers
With these wild drops, the cloud's bell-flowers,
Rarer far is the fragrance cast
From her kind life, the song that her lightest
Word awakens is unsurpassed
By birds that call their heaven the brightest;
What shall I say to her, my Marie?
" Work I will, for work is good,
And work is health, that's understood;
Pity it steals one's liberty.
Out on the land, or carting lime,
One may not hope for oceans of time;
But in the twilight, when the dew
Begins to rise, and labour's through,
I'll meet her beside the refinery gate,
And we'll walk by the tuilerie pond;
It will not be me who is a moment late,
We'll get to the mill and beyond;
Sway, sweet hawthorn; swing, proud reed;
Lumber along, slow wheels;
And you, old rascally mare, proceed,
Remember who gets your meals."

The south-west sighed, the sky still poured,
Perfume and gleam and coolness flowed
About the colonnaded road,
And still new skylarks soared;

Blue fluted tiles on the town-end shrine
Shimmered with summer's splash of wet;
And the waggon and boy atop of it set
Passed where we camped; the luck was mine,
To catch from the face of the boy
One record of faultless joy.

So singing then the vernal rain
Came waterfalling over the plain,
So leapt the pure triumphant breeze—
And so one secret oversang these!

THE TREE IN THE GOODS YARD

So sigh, that hearkening pasts arouse
In the magic circle of your boughs,—
So timelessly, on sound's deep sea,
Sail your unfurled melody,
     My small dark Tree.

Who set you in this smoky yard
None tells me; it might seem too hard
A fate for a tree whose place should be
With a sounding proud-plumed company
     By a glittering sea.

And yet you live with liking here,
Are well, have some brocade to wear,
And solitary, mysteriously
Revoice light airs as sighs, which free
     Tombed worlds for me.

FARM BAILIFF

I

Enter the man, right farmer's countenance: part
Is peasant, you may say, or some Dutch boor
Whom Teniers painted. View that face athwart,
What aristocracy! At the inn's tall door
He needs not stoop to-day—that much claims Age;
And here's his chair, and here we have him young,
And sixty years ago is an open page;
This year's keen spring speaks with his sprightly tongue.

With hand and pipe to point how topics turn,
He prompts our sense of things, though words alone
Like his tell all at once; his day's concern
" As otherwhile," is how green life comes on.
Pease have " put out their kit's claws. Five or six,"
He nods, " are man enough to reach the sticks."

II

Old Albert—Father Cheeseman,—so all spoke
In latter years of you: I did not fear
So soon to come again and you not here,
Our small town altered by a surly stroke
Of death, and the good book of many a year
Suddenly closed. New times, new wisdoms, new
Characters come, I know, but mourn for you.

In this the home of husbandry when first
I viewed all skill with young admiring zeal,
The pride of man and beast, of plough and wheel,
The soil, the seed, the yield so kindly nursed,
All that the country's casket could reveal

263

Of living treasure, foremost did you stand,
Great husbandman, master of widespread land.

Say it came natural—so yourself might say,
And nature's self could hardly have a sense
More sure and constant than has now gone hence
With you, for all that happens night and day,
And shine and shower, and tiny and immense,
In the ancient world of sap and grain and gourd,
Of dog and hog, of worm and bee and bird.

But not alone from these your oneness shines;
You had your pride, but it was on your lip
Most when remembering feats of sportsmanship,
Grand cricket, utmost prey of rods and lines,
Something of bowls, and then of spur and whip,
And autumn guns,—but cricket maybe most,
—Still in the slips I see you take your post.

Why, the small boy's first evening in the nets,
With bat almost above his ears, you came
To start him rightly in your classic game,
And lobbed the slow spun ball that always gets
The hopeful one—and first he tasted fame;
In Paradise I think you bowl so still,
Your art is feared by teams beyond the hill.

We follow, Father; and, as you approve,
We hasten slowly, as we are allowed.
Your old friends, daily grayer and more bowed,
Mildly along the lonelier pathway move,
And gathering, few now, chase the general cloud
By borrowing light you bore when you talked there
From the pink bud till orchard boughs are bare.

A PRAYER FOR THE BIRDS

Rise from your grave, Charles Waterton,*
And range the world, and charm together
Birds of every note and feather,
And lead that varied troop as one
Into some safe and secret dell
Where they with you and hope may dwell,—

Some solitude of water and wood
Such as you made for earlier singers,
The least that flit, the powerful wingers,
Long ago, when life was good;
Some home like yours, old Yorkshire squire,
To shelter all this shattered choir.

For truly man in his grim concerns
Deserves them not, and hardly heeds them,
Laughs to be counselled that he needs them;
So that when dawn cool-limbed returns
Instead of her minstrelsy all she hears
Are a few far voices laden with fears.

AFTER THE BOMBING

My hesitant design it was, in a time when no man feared,
To make a poem on the last poor flower to have grown on
    the patch of land
Where since a gray enormous stack of shops and offices
    reared
Its bulk as though to eternity there to stand.

* Charles Waterton, 1782-1865, used his estate at Walton Hall, Yorkshire, as a bird sanctuary. Mr. Richard Aldington has published the most recent account of him.

Moreover I dreamed of a lyrical verse to welcome another
  flower,
The first to blow on that hidden site when the concrete
  block should cease
Gorging the space; it could not be mine to foretell the
  means, the hour,
But nature whispered something of a longer lease.

We look from the street now over a breezy wilderness of
  bloom,
Now, crowding its colours between the sills and cellars,
  hosts of flame
And foam, pearl-pink and thunder-red, befriending the
  makeshift tomb
Of a most ingenious but impermanent claim.

FROM THE FLYING-BOAT

Into the blue undisturbable main
    The blue streams flow,
    In time they flow
Out of chasms vaporous, spurs far-whitening, winding
  gorges
    Woven of snow;
    This height we gain.
    The country enlarges.

There the mountain cloudland, and far at the verge
    Cliff-cloudlands upsurge;
Here, countless, an archipelago—
How the islands tower in their strength, quincunxes so
May confront such eyes as understand them, down below;
    And yet up here I hardly know,

So little is this brilliant change, although
It extends in kingdom bright, so fast we go
Into apparent eternity—but, truth is, all things flow.

And now I am mounted aloft and have taken a wing,
Into the blue undisturbable oceaning,
More prospect than pyramidal Egypt, or perhaps the
Mountains of the Moon could bring,
With whom shall we meet in this place?
Why hides He His face?

JOY AND MARGARET

My darling, what a power is yours
To make me weep, after such years;
For twenty-seven years at least
Are gone since your brief coming ceased,—
And still you force my hopeless tears
And still your fate dwarfs all my wars.

Joy was your name and in that choice
You from the first were all consent,
And soon as infants ever smile,
My little one, would you beguile
Your company, and innocent
Found out your art to make rejoice.

Not for a second might I dream
That you could pass, that you would fade,
So lifeward strove your wish, and you
Daily my dear companion grew;
But in one day the seizing Shade
Cut you from me, outwent the extreme.

267

That was the strangest thing, my sweet,
Nor can I rise from what it spelled,
For while you lay in that gray clutch
You heard my step, you knew my touch,
And looked cross wonder that I failed
To shield you from the cold and heat.

Look not thus ever, tiny wretch,
Dear child of long ago; we bring
A second self with whom your span
May round, with Margaret now you can
Make fun of things, feed, call and sing,
Tease, tantalize, adore, bewitch.

THE HALTED BATTALION

One hour from far returns: Each man we had
Was well content that hour, the time, the place,
And war's reprieve combining. Each good face
Stood easy, and announced life not too bad.

Then almost holy came a light, a sense,
And whence it came I did not then inquire;
Simple the scene,—a château wall, a spire,
Towpath, swing-bridge, canal with bulrush-fence.

Still I, as dreamer known, that morning saw
The others round me taken with a dream.
I wondered since that never one of them
Recalls it; but how should they? We who draw
Picture and meaning are the dreamless, we
Are sentinels of time while the rest are free.

It is not wholly past, the time enrolled
In registers grown old; those records lie
Outside the playhouse of the inward eye,
And life's a story not so simply told.
We speak of ghosts, as those who from some fold
Of death escape, and as cold shades flit by;
We ponder change, watch in our lifetime die
A multitude of scenes; yet some will hold
These terms of time, ghosts, change and death unmeaning
Compared with that deep presence of all in one
Which through our common notions intervening
Adds magic to the moonlight, gives the sun
Another glory; and quiet place and day
Disclose for a flash the boundless, timeless play.

BYRONIANA

(I) KIRKE WHITE AT WILFORD

*Unhappy White! while life was in its spring,
And thy young Muse just waved her joyous wing.*
BYRON

Here came the mild boy loving loneliness
So long as he might hear the friendly din
Of happy people, see the sunlit tent
And dancing-ring apart from the distress,
Watch the sails travel along the mirroring Trent;
But all as toys compared with that within
His dying breast, the eternal grace ensued
With daily resignation, hours of zeal

For fate that came so cruelly at first,
And now by courage and chosen solitude
Made sweet as Maybloom. Here his sense immersed
In that loved fragrance made no doubt to feel
The spirit breeze, called death, with greater love.
So passed the youth who sang of Clifton Grove,
And cannot quite be banished though the age
With power-house and with colliery overbrow
The churchyard of his musing pilgrimage,
And few chimes dance in the breeze that flies here now.

(II) NEWSTEAD

Past the mines and past the workshops
Runs the road with lodge and cover,
Till the big lake glitters at us
Where that old lord would manœuvre
Ships of war in mimic fight;
But on him rests no modern light,
Only on the younger rover
Who with all Europe had his fun.
Surely Byron in this sun
Will soon be stepping bat in hand
Across his lawns, with lordly friends
Whose classic tags we guess while he
Poises among them Grecianly
Or he will fish for perch alone,
And from high windows see you one
Of simplest beauty scan the land,

And where he sits her survey ends;
But only as a joyous ranger,
Pausing here for May and June,
Comes the glorious creature Byron,
Cuts his reed and pipes his tune,
Mocks the monks and fools the girls—
And out and away to the great stage hurls.

HIGH ELMS, BRACKNELL

Two buds we took from thousands more
    In Shelley's garden overgrown,
    Beneath our roof they are now full-blown,
A royal pair, a scarlet twain
    Through whose warm lives our thoughts explore
    Back through long years to come at one
Which Shelley loved in sun or rain.

Fleeting's the life of these strange flowers,
    Enchanting poppies satin-frilled,
    Dark-purple hearts, yet these rebuild
A distant world, a summer dead*
    Millions of poppy-lives ere ours,
    And Shelley's visionary towers
Come nearer in their Indian red;

Not but some shadow of despair
    In this dark purple ominous
    From that high summer beckons us;
And such a shadow, such a doom
    Was lurking in the garden there.
    We could not name the incubus,
Save that it haunted Shelley's home.

Was it that through the same glass door
    With weary heart, uncertain why,
    But first discerning love can die,
Harriet had moved alone and slow;
    Or Shelley in the moonlight bore
    The cold curt word Necessity
From poppies that had seemed to know?

* In 1813.

271

Then tracing the lost path between
　　The herbs and flowers and wilderness,
　　Whose was the phantom of our guess
Drawn by that quiet deserted pond
　　With little boat, now scarcely seen
　　For tears or bodings? Whose distress
Darkened the watery diamond?

ON READING A MAGAZINE EDITED
BY OSCAR WILDE

Once on a time before I heard
Of your life-history half a word
I read some verses wherein you
With rural heart and liking drew
Rich meadow pictures, caught the sounds
Of flock and flight in dewy grounds;
And much I honoured such a man, whose natural joy sang
　　so,
And wished to see you tracing the streams where I alone
　　would go.

Perhaps I missed your main intent
But ever before me charmed you went,
And in most beautiful design
You set the things I counted mine.
The shoals in pools with morning rays
Resplendent held us both at gaze,
And if none else delighted in the dancing dragon-fly
And nesting pigeon in the ash, you did, and I knew why.

Soon sent from water-lily haunts,
And where the honeysuckle flaunts,
I heard your name—but withering fame
Hurled savage echoes of the same,

And called you false, and called you worse,
Sneered if it even recalled your verse;
But ever in my secret mind I could not think it true,
And when the wit had spent its shot, I still went back to
  you.

Now turning these fair pages, still
I find you on the Muses' hill;
Not singing here, but with fixed thought
On things by art of all kinds wrought,
Generous, informed, deep-finding, plain,
Sparkling in points, broad-bright in the main;
Hence in these later years I bring this homage to your
  shade,
With tears enough, but final joy that what you were has
  stayed.

THE BLUEPRINT

Will you then build us a house that will vie with the houses
  we know,
A hauntable house, a dwelling for dreams,
And where things may sometimes play truant and rest
Out of the glare of constant employ, and the test
Of this or that moment's requirings and schemes?
A house that will murmur in age, " My children, long
  ago . . ."?

Will you too fashion a church that's awake to the April
  showers
Where the merry angels are ready to wing
In the painted roof with praise and prayer
To one who being heaven's King
Is splendour enthroned over earth's dim air?
A church where the altar lilies appear as the soul's new
  flowers?

So you will find us your friends, and the rest of our market
    town
Shall be yours to create, folk's delight to possess,
Where the image of sweet content shall dwell
Not in one carven form but in graciousness
Of all from weathercock to well,
And sunbeam and shadow bring each all day a beauty
    down.

INVOCATION WRITTEN IN SPRING
1944

Come, angel most beloved, come, most rejected;
    Flower from afar (for far thou hast fled),
        Visit us again;
We had thy grace before when least expected,
    And those who seemed already dead
        Crept from horror's den

Into the morning of thy yet sad smile;
    Small wonder if thy cheek was misty and pallid
        Where such ruin lay,
Or if thy music grew not full awhile,
    Till all the azure-mountained, verdant-valleyed
        World remembered day.

Visit us so again, entrancing lover
    Of time, love, hope and harvest; find
        Way and point to come,
And while men hardly dream night could be over,
    Unveil cool mercy, sing the note so kind,
        Change black hell to home.

THE PORTRAIT

Will you make witchcraft holy? For your eyes
Which call to mind some spring and shrine of old
By saint's name known—so innocently rise
Those looks to mine—are yet of power to fold
In a strong spell and strange all that I am;
And on your lips, that are truth's character,
I dwell with danger, catching thence a flame
That dances wild to lure me anywhere
So you are there. The laws of time and place,
Outwitted by your music and your light,
Guide me not then, the thrall of your fair face;
And though you bid me from all else take flight
I go rejoicing—but your spirit's gaze
Will lead to sunlit deeds and charm to honour's ways.

SERENA

From dark to fiery, mute to loud
The tempest days of autumn change;
A glory then on gloom will crowd,
Time grows electrical and strange—
And sometimes known in you I bless
Such flashing powerful changefulness.

And yet I bless besides caprice
That heavenly quietude, my dear,
That pure serene, that lulling peace
Which knows no haste, and dreams no fear,
Like evening skies in countries where
Great belfries shine in golden air.

This peace that looks from your wide eyes
And on your lip rests, even your hand,
Is such an earthly paradise
That I delighted understand
What life could be for humankind
Were peace so pictured to their mind.

RIVAL FEASTS

On the roof-ridge stops the sparrow to enjoy his bit of
    bread,
For once a clean white morsel,—and a not ungrateful bird;
And this side of the window I stay happily in bed,
But like him have an appetite—mine, for the written word;
        And I am better far supplied
        With all these volumes at my side.

I much admire his honest haste, and sense of what is good;
Besides he seems to know that this may be the last calm
    day
For months to come; that gleam of sun is not misunder-
    stood—
After the night's black gale the year must sharply fall away;
        So I discern my reading spell
        Is brief and must be managed well.

Like him I cannot wholly choose my special nourishment,
But providence has given enough, and of the truest grain;
Here, come to hand no matter how, is infinite content;
Except a thing which irks not him; perhaps it is no gain
        Instead of one choice single dish
        To have a dozen if you wish.

Meanwhile I feed almost as fast: here's merit old and
  new,—
The book of life by Chaucer, and this latest de la Mare;
Dame Una's tale of Dickens, and the Dickens Sala drew;
Birrell on wise and foolish things, or Fielding, in the chair;
      And, now I see my bird is flown,
      I feast on Browning's best alone.

HAMMOND (ENGLAND)

A CRICKETER

Since our most beautiful and subtle game
First grew from England's leas and levels green,
In turn its champions in their genius came—
Men who had but to walk into the scene
To be its masters; in each magic name,
A generation felt the whole serene
Enchantment of this play, this art, this test
Of character and skill a thousand ways expressed.

The observed of all observers long ago,
The models of young hearts dreaming of glory,
Great in all lights that fell upon the show
And tournament of cricket, leave the story
To greater still; its scope and problems grow
Beyond their use, nor would their ghosts be sorry;
Perhaps that company of kings of cricket
Have means of watching well their followers at the wicket.

Ourselves have watched the classics of our days
With little fear of past or future boast;
In our own sunshine we have men to praise
Above the lordliest Hambledonian ghost;
Round the wide world the bright pavilions blaze
With modern honours,—where to honour most

277

In Bradman's era is our question; then,
Hammond is taking guard. There stands our man of men

Not to have seen Hammond in such an hour
Is not to know the stature of true sport,
The quiet instancy of natural power,
Completeness, fluent action in each sort
Of cricket's needs; how this command will tower
Above the skilful rest all minds report;
Not to have seen him leaves us unaware
What cricket swiftness, judgment, foresight truly are.

So comes he to the field, and of his sway
And sceptre is by now much more assured
Than dynasties in fields where nations play
With danger; call his kingdom Bon Accord,
And mark the complete master to this day,
Still studious of the least thing unexplored,
True to first principles, approving ever
Modesty's patient eye for other men's endeavour.

Cricket's Sir Christopher! his trophies rise
Above the skyline of so many a year
As Wren's clear steeples blazon London skies,
And in their eminence not once appear
Envious of it; their architect descries
The personal sign, content of his career
Interprets what once charmed him as a boy—
The game's delight, the infinite art, event and joy.

CHANGE AND SONG

No, do not tell me; have I not conceded
   That times have changed and verse like mine grown old,
That new thoughts need shapes other than ours needed?
   It is the eternal scheme: the years unfold
Their bidden novelty. Times go by turns,
But each fresh triumph spells some hurts and spurns.

There are no Muses now, there are no Graces,
   No angels on the clouds—but I was young
While still some ray from these in kindly places
   Made us look twice, and, as it seemed, the tongue
Of that which knows not death was understood
From dawn's great hill, from twilight's watchful wood.

No trick of mine it was that clear and cool
   By the arched grey bridge of summer-merry streams,
A song of centuries winged my walk to school.
   That song went with me through unguessed extremes.
The soul of that ghost song I cannot tell
In words; its visitings have served me well.

Is old earth tired? Is sunflowered earth grown old,
   Like verse the voice of many who died young?
Seemingly so. These now at prime behold,
   They tell me, nothing of what soared and sung
Like Phoebus for swift Shakespeare, haunted shy
Where his friend the teamster urged his horses by.

Doubt might cloud dense upon me, but I hear
   Goethe and Shelley, Melville and poor Clare
With many another whose track from spring to sere
   Now flushed with May, now glinted flintily bare,
I hear them answering that same morning song,
And heavenly silence more than belfry-strong.

Beloved museful singers heard by me
   Through all the chequered years, and darling-treasured
Visions of sunlit clouds, that melody
   And faith of yours, unquestioned and unmeasured,
Bears me on still, and will, and nothing ends
And no joy withers while such song befriends.

RUNNING STREAM

Whether this beck has self and personal pride
Or is mere accident of sequent streaminess,
Drop following drop, " wandering companionless,"
    Let sage, saint, seer decide.

I watch its course; my life that has loved so many
Wildbrooks flowing, never had answer from any
To question of mine. Away they hastened,
Away with a music; but not a note of it lessoned
My curious sense, nor said if the stream was grown
More than a travelling of waters drawn together
From gully and moledrain by contour, chance and weather;
None revealed if a spirit indwelt their bubbling adown.

Here is the breast-high hollowed stone;
I ask him too, does he know any deep
Secret; the stone pretends to sleep;
The small stream channelling on remains unknown.
The mosses on the towering stone,
The fern, the waterfly, each one,
Stands in some rank of conscious life,—each one
    Delightful stream,
Sparkling with hope and pleasure do you run,
Or were the Naiads creatures of a dream?

There are faces here to-day,
    Just a few,
Which would make old Romans say,
    " Why, it's you!
Still a-brishing sprig and thorn
In the thorp where you were born,
    Where we burnished our array—
        And withdrew."

That wayside shrewdness there,
    He indeed
Seems to have all time to spare:
    The old breed,
Short and stubby, young and old,
Starting up in field and fold,
    Of earth-secrets given the share
        For his need.

There are corners here to-day,
    One or two,
Where a wildflower can decay
    As it grew;
Where the foxgloves at their time
Towards the honeysuckles climb
    And the snow-soft daisies stay
        Snow-showers through.

Here are country sports as yet
    You may spy:
Spanlong rabbits quite forget
    Danger's eye;

Those may bracken deeps preserve.
Dancing midges swirl and swerve,
    And a thousand starlings met
        Race on high.

    It may be the last of all
        For all these,
And this sagging rosebrown wall,
        Willow-trees,
Hut and hovel, green and pond,
Ere we dream may be beyond,
    And our peasant past recall;
        It may please
One who marks the sparrow's fall
        To save these.

THE SEASON REOPENS

" A tower we must have, and a clock in the tower,
Looking over the tombs, the tithebarn, the bower;
The inn and the mill, the forge and the hall
And the loamy sweet level that loves bat and ball."

So a gray tower we have, and some centuried trees
Have arisen to share what its belfry-light sees,—
The apple-plats richest in spring-song of all,
Kitchen-gardens, one field where they take bat and ball.

Our stream, with its moments of dance in the sun
Where the willows allow, runs and ever will run
At the cleft of the orchards, along the soft fall
Of the pasture where tourneys became bat and ball.

And now where the confident cuckoo takes flight
Over buttercups kindled in millions last night,
A labourer leans on the stackyard's low wall,
With the hens bothering round him, and dreams bat and
    ball:

Till the meadow is quick with the champions who were,
And he hears his own shouts when he first trotted there,
Long ago: all gone home now; but here they come all!
Surely these are the same who now bring bat and ball?

ASSAULTING WAVES

The north wind vexes the gravel-pit, shrill from a sky of
    stone,
Of stone that moves immense; and pounded and hewn and
    blown
The stained lake surges and crests, races with foaming throat
To explode like waves of the sea abrupt on the dredgers'
    boat.

And further hurling the swarm jumps at the cavernous
    shore
To be shattered but still to upleap numberless, full of war.
What seek you, puny assailants? To swallow the kingdom,
    the earth?
Conquerors look you to grow, being airy frenzy's birth?

283

WATER-MEADOW EVENING

After the great blue day, the confident light
With every thistle-head in perfect sight,
Path, step and stile clear-carved, you see Old Night
      Begin to shade the river-glade,
        And Fear return:
Or, if not Fear, then call this only white
Water-mist, hovering head-high, merely mist,
Of which the calm intelligence might learn
All the particulars; but to be kissed
By it, or her, has never seemed to us
Who know this coming less than perilous.

When evening falls, they speed beyond these damps
Who need, to cottages or cautious camps;
Across the leas I mark their racing lamps
      And lit-up trees, across the leas,
        But who are they?
None of our parish, not so much as tramps
Who hoof our lanes—for these the ghost walks not.
These may all hurtle or drift and go their way.
The river Circe will not touch their throat.
Others who own these grounds, or feel they do
By noonday use, suspect her rendezvous.

Our paths, our stones across rush-pools, our posts
Are easy, were it not for Night and ghosts;
Like doubt occurs with well-known lofts and oasts
      When good light wastes and blackness hastes
        And silver-white
The unspeaking mist is moving for accosts
About familiarity's altered ground.
We shall not travel that brief mile to-night.
Even we have read the poet's " mists unsound."

Or we shall tarry till her pale walk is done
And ripples sparkle to the unclouded moon.

YOUNG FIELDMOUSE

Beseechingly this little thing—
Strayed from deep grass and breezy scented Spring
Into undreamed perils which have struck it down
Already—here in the den of the town
Takes refuge and finds pause in your warm palms
And dares to peer about, till its terror calms.

There is no hope for such a mangled mite,
Whose life depends on what we cannot guess,
Or nourishment or surgery; none the less
Indulge this child, this stranger with eye so bright,
So dim—so bright again, for love can do
Much, and the illusion is as good (in its time) as true.

We try our makeshifts, one by one they pass;
It tries; but in the end, in the long green grass,
The infant body stiffens, and the frame
Of the universe, to us, dies a little with the same.

THOSE WHO FIRST ENCOURAGED US

Sweet sing the verse, while this we sing:
The lovely frankness long ago
From eyes of black or eyes of blue,
The noble dreams of you, and you,
Compassionate; you might not know
To-day, that you inspired us so.
Sweet be my verse while you I sing!

May I not fail, though old I grow,
In grace toward youth, and honouring
And thanks for that which gentleness
And grace continue to impress;
Be yours the music, yours the spring
Which tune and colour everything;
This be my blessing, fare you so!

THE FOND DREAM

Here's the dream I love.
  Stay, old Sleep, allow me this
  Yet one moment, godlike bliss.
Here's the dream I love.

Tell us then that dream?
  O, it's nothing, nothing at all.
  But I was walking young and small
In a scene like a happy dream.

What especial scene?
  None especial: pure blue sky,
  Cherry orchards a brook runs by,
And an old church crowns the scene.

Only that? If so,
  All would be well; but, dreams have changed.
  Dreamers are banished, joys estranged.
I wake; it is not so.

EARLY IDEAS REAWAKENED

What ghosts are these? What hope could bring
These faltering shades on midnight's wing
      To meet this older me?

Their forms are indistinct, they fly
As vapours in the moonlight sky,
      They yet turn back on me

As if an eye of grief—and hark!
Still as they come the sleeping dark
      Stirs to brief minstrelsy.

From mounts of light besides they carry
Shows of still-soaring towers, but tarry
      Never that I may see

More than my blame, when first they came
Offering me all, would I but claim—
      Had I but eyes to see.

THE FARMHOUSE FAMILY

I ran along, I sang alone;
      in a moment was as free and far
From the house of childhood as if I had flown
      to a cloud, a mountain or a star;
      That was the morning of May.

And round the ring the hours took wing,
      with some shrill notes and plenty sweet,
My tasks and liberties flying with them,
      in solitude now and now in street.
      So passed the willing day:

Till mists and shadows estranged the meadows,
        and birds in hedges obeyed the god
Of dawn and dusk, and I too hastened
        home from the river with line and rod
    To the lamp of love's sure ray.

So all we go, and what of the night?
        it was safe smooth interval, hardly felt,
Till the blossom and song burst forth new-bright,
        and the country genius freshly dealt
    To each child a glittering way.

H-BOMB

" If they roosh on like this they'll ruin all,"
Said my old uncle resting on his spade.
" Now in that other war, when you was small,
I dare say you remember how they sprayed
(One summer night) or chance you didn't wake,
Our cricket-ground with bombs—big holes they make.

" And them there bombs, six of them in a line,
Lifted the glass out of our blessed church;
The old East Window went,—the new one's fine,
But nought to that: where Jesus used to perch
On that plump donkey bound for Egypt, yes,
That was a work of art,—the donk no less.

" But they're blown up, and Wise Men blown up too,—
And what's the score?" I answered, " Hutton's in!
He's going well." My uncle: " Good for you.
What about Hobbs?" " Hobbs?". " Where have you a-
    bin?"
Still he forgave me, and allowed me this:
" You've come in a thin time, my little Ciss."

And then,—" If they go on they'll upset all,
They and their funny bomb. They nearly did
The last time. Up to then I bowled a ball
That came back quick; but where that bomb-hole hid
It never did again. Things aren't the same.
I tell you, girl, they've no sense of a game."

I watched the old man, and I held my tongue.
He was so simple, and I was so young.

THE SUSSEX DOWNS

Calm and curious, kindly, great,
    You seemed up there
      To contemplate
    Our trundling lives with time to spare.

Venture who would, so would not I
    On your broad breast
      Where only sky
    And shepherd patriarchs should rest.

Highland lane and hilltop wood
    Near home we saw
      As friends; you stood
    As gods, while temples still could awe.

IN MEMORY OF ROBERT NICHOLS

Truth may not be less sharp because " 'tis true."
    We knew it all the time: soon said, "we knew."
But till time brings it home to me and you,

It floats a starlit cloud, a ship of dreams.
Far wide, with beautiful unnoticed gleams.
That Spring is brief and Spring is swift, this seems

Commonly known, and who has failed to be
Grounded in this gray truth from infancy?
Yet few shall ever conceive it vitally

Till something happens, as this something will.
Best is the height proved by the ascended hill.
The starved know hunger; pleasant vices kill.

Thinking of Spring, in all adventurous youth,
I knew it laughs in joy of its own growth,
Fades, falls: what poetry spelt us not that truth?

You, challenging companion, fragile, strong,
Ambitious champion and recluse of song,
Came Spring-like on me,—did I ask, " How long?"

" The bell is sounding down in Dedham Vale,"
And this night's snow loads merry Robert's grave.
I half forgot it; in my fairy-tale
He was afoot as once, a minstrel brave,
From the dawn's field-lark to dusk's nightingale.
But cold truth strikes. Farewell. Let tempest rave.

C. E. B.

OB. NOVEMBER 1951

Are all your eighty years defined at last
In so few terms? the chair and bookshelves by,
The latest pipe, the cared-for shoes, the stick
(Long since presented with some public thanks)

As good as new, but latterly less astir;
The post and railway times penned as of old
Beautifully for the fireside wall?
Not even your cricket-bag attending now,
Not the bream-ledger, nor the hopground picture,
Nor one school register, nor book of chants,
Though these will come to hand as days press on,
When your monastic face that seemed to pass
In a high procession from our local world,
Set on some boyhood vision, never uttered
To any but one, will be but village clay.

FRANK WORLEY,
D.C.M.

JULY 1954

There was no death but you would face it
    Even in your youth;
No riddle of life but you would grace it
    With your brave truth.

To share, to give, to make privation
    No trouble at all,
To honour all wise occupation
    And duty's call,—

Such was your spirit, Frank, dear fighter
    Foremost for peace,
Through whom even sunniest hours grew brighter
    And dark thoughts cease;

To whom heaven gave reward best showing
    Whereto you strove:
Old and young friendships overflowing
    And a home of love.

" If aught of native verse in far-on years
May hope, O pensive soul, to win your smile
    Like your own hauntings where
    You found what poets find,

Where lilied Arun all the lovelier ran
Because the ghost of generous Otway laid,
    It seemed, a hand on yours,
    And you were not alone,—

Where thatch and chimney in long-dying light
Maintained the village's half-pagan faith,
    Where sheepbells rang as true
    As from the spire's low louvre

The bell of Christ; or if along the downs
Melodious morning led some company
    Of those whose spring it was,
    And one who to your mind

Would where she walked make all the year glad Spring,—
Collins, receive my words, illumine these
    With your compassion, change
    Defect with your bright love.

For I am of your region, and our name
Passed in your town, some of that name chance-met,
    A parish-clerk, a boy
    Poring on books, a bride.

By Lavant side, and on the sleet-stormed miles
Of lonely road, or where old carven stone
    Regains its eloquence
    In the last gleam of day,

I too have made my journeys; now the light
Of memory rests on love and friendship known
    When every hour called forth
    Some relic of your fame.

Be mine to rove before my darkness falls
In your still cloistered city, yet once more,
    At your own door to stand,
    And your kind influence own."

UNRECORDED

Once on a time might you or I
Hail one called Shakespeare passing by,
" Accost," and if the hour were fit
Engage him to surrender it
To leisured inn-talk, which among
Something delightfully had sprung
Of Shakespeare's which is not here now
    In any book.
    Lost as his look.
Such chances offered, men avow,
    Once on a time.

Long, long ago it was not hard
To loiter by a playhouse yard,
And—see! young Marlowe entering there
With a countenance all fire and air,
The eye that launched a thousand sails
Of fancies tongued like nightingales,
The likeness that is nowhere now,
    So much desired.
    The face inspired.
There were these chances, all avow,
    Long, long ago.

293

The other day, was it not, my friend?
We saw a face, did comprehend
Nature and art; we knew the flower
We came on; and we grudged an hour.
Half-listening, half-regarding so,—
And spring returns, and new flowers blow.
It was only, seize it on the bough—
The blossom craved,
Which was not saved.
Such chances smiled there, we allow,
The other day.

AS BOSWELL RECORDS

" Not to drink wine," said The Rambler,
" is a great deduction from life."
Well have the sages perceived
truths many and principles sound;
Well have they found the right words for them,
they or the world and his wife;
But nothing more clear than this truth
from Sam Johnson was ever yet found.

" It may be necessary,"
said the Moralist, eyeing his friend
Necessity, goddess perhaps,
knew no ardent disciple in him.
These words had a lower tone,
for the thought ran, " Heaven defend
That time should produce this compulsion;
fill up, and fill to the brim."

Many are the sayings of the wise,
               and a long day finds their grace,
Solace and strength, the light
               on the chaos, the truce to the strife;
But never may Maxim or Rule
               excel that calm call to the race.
" Not to drink wine," said our Johnson,
               " is a great deduction from life."

AT THE GREAT WALL OF CHINA

Perched in a tower of this ancestral Wall,
Of man's huge warlike works the hugest still,
We scan its highway lashing hill to hill,
We dream its form as though we saw it all;
Where these few miles to thousands grow, and yet
Ever the one command and genius haunt
Each stairway, sally-port, loop, parapet,
In mute last answer to the invader's vaunt.

But I half know at this bleak turret here,
In snow-dimmed moonlight where sure answers quail,
This new-set sentry of a long dead year,
This boy almost, trembling lest he may fail
To espy the ruseful raiders, and his mind
Torn with sharp love of the home left far behind.

CHIMES AT MIDNIGHT

Saints from the old world sounding on
With music fill my midnight mind;
The task I tried is quickly gone,
I see where I was blind.
Glad sons of light, by your accord
Even from the pit I stand restored.

Now may I sing with something young
Reborn in answer to your choir,
And let that seraph touch my tongue
With such divine desire
As passed just now through this slow frame,
And uttered all in one great Name.

VISION

from the French of Eugène Manuel. Parisian, born 1823

I

In a somewhat sadder dream
I saw two cottages, very much the same,
Whence in the dim
Two voices, plaintive voices, came.

Both dwellings were veiled
In one of those good valleys where plenty smiled,
But war had compelled
Thence many a father, many a child.

Winter-time;—winter-days swell
Longing for absent folk, for those loved well,
When the bitter bill
Of the frost stabs the wounded, lying pale.

Now slowly the snow laid
Flakes and flakes upon the branches dead;
Where the wind sighed
Long at door-chinks of the stead.

All road-ways empty:
The crows through the dense mist flying intently
In companies, scenting,
Beyond the horizon, a singular plenty.

I saw two hearths,
Much alike, burning twigs or peat or furze,
Two mothers, shaking with nerves,
Thinking about the distant wars:

Two hearts straining
In anguish, loss of caresses yet beginning;
Now duty enchaining
Worried their thoughts, and humble complaining.

In spirit they moved—
No letter comes, none that might have relieved—
Where their sons were involved:
From wars, mothers never but woundings received.

And one made moan,
Piteous in her language and in our own,
" Mein kind." Do I go on?
" Mon fils," so murmured the other one.

297

U

In the instant of which I have told,
I heard amid the frightful battle field,
Striving with pain, the dulled
Voice of two children, equally old.

It was winter, and day dying;
The cannons had just stopped brawling and braying,
All about in the graying
You saw Frenchmen and Germans lying.

And the snow raced on the gale
Over the woods to those pale
Foreheads; the deep chill
Night was pierced with a general wail.

These two soldiers looked alike,
Dying, when life would be their right luck,
Their poor limbs shook
With the wind's or the rimefrost's blue stroke.

Failing the two
Felt their blood past staunching flow,
While the flocking crow
Circled above the arena of snow.

They were dying in a ravine,
Each in the ultimate pain,
Each stared in vain
For the stretchers in moving line.

The strange dream of things that are past
That precedes us at the very last
Gave to either, blest,
The vision of that he called his best.

These two in the moment of
Death's passage both tell their first love,
Children so leave
At all times their appeal above.

And one in a monotone
Piteous in his tongue, and in our own,—
" Mutter, Mutter." Do I go on?
" Maman, Maman," said the other one.

INDEX OF TITLES

301

INDEX OF FIRST LINES

311

When now at this stern depth and shade of soul, 132
When on the green the rag-tag game had stopt, 69
When you are by, I think of time as boys, 245
Whether this beck has self and personal pride, 280
While by the rosebud gay you stood, and revelled in the multitude, 247
While few men praise and hardly more defend, 217
While I sit penning plans of dead affairs, 169
While on my cheek the sour and savage wind, 161
Who knows not that sweet gloom in spring, 121
Why are they dead? Is Adam's seed so strong, 223
Wide as the world is, music abounds, 160
Willing to give whatever art I know, 232
Will you make witchcraft holy? For your eyes, 275
Will you then build us a house that will vie with the houses we know, 273
With blind eyes meeting the mist and moon, 134
With coat like any mole's, as soft and black, 71
With half a hundred sudden loops and coils, 217
With rural admixture of shrill and sweet, 19
With what delight the south's large rain, 260
Yes, I still remember, 209